BIRDS & BLOOMS®

Birding & Gardening Secrets

BIRDS & BLOOMS

Contributing Art Director Kathryn Finney
Contributing Editor Kirsten Sweet
Editor/_Birds & Blooms_ Stacy Tornio
Art Director/_Birds & Blooms_ Sue Myers
Senior Editor/_Birds & Blooms_ Crystal Rennicke
Copy Chief Deb Warlaumont Mulvey
Assistant Editor/Digital Danielle Calkins
Editorial Assistant Lorie West
Copy Editors Joanne Weintraub, Dulcie Shoener
Production Coordinator Dena Ahlers
Layout Coordinator Dana Borremans
Birding Expert George Harrison
Horticulture Expert Melinda Myers
Contributing Editor Sally Roth

Vice President, Editor In Chief Catherine Cassidy
Executive Editor/Home & Garden Heather Lamb
Creative Director/Home & Garden Sharon K. Nelson

Photo Studio Business Manager Kimberly Gohr
Photo Coordinator Trudi Bellin
Assistant Photo Coordinator Mary Ann Koebernik

Vice President, Executive Editor/Books Heidi Reuter Lloyd
Senior Editor/Books Mark Hagen
Associate Editor/Books Ellie Martin Cliffe

North American Chief Marketing Officer Lisa Karpinski
Vice President/Book Marketing Dan Fink

The Reader's Digest Association, Inc.
President and Chief Executive Officer Mary G. Berner
President, North American Affinities Suzanne M. Grimes

©2011 Reiman Media Group, LLC
5400 S. 60th St., Greendale WI 53129-1404

International Standard Book Number:
0-89821-873-X
978-0-89821-873-2

Library of Congress Control Number: 2010942922

On the Cover: American goldfinch, Marie Read

For questions, write to:
Birds & Blooms Customer Service
P.O. Box 5294
Harlan IA 51593-0794;
Call toll-free: 800-344-6913;
e-mail: rpsubscustomercare@custhelp.com.
Visit our website at birdsandblooms.com.

Sometimes it's not what you know, but who you know.

In the world of birding and gardening, this really rings true. Think about it. You can read all the birding books in the world to learn how to stop squirrels, but the best advice usually comes from a seasoned birder who has developed his or her own foolproof method for combating the furry little critters.

The same is true for gardening. You can follow planting instructions word for word, but it's Grandma's advice or a local gardener's tip that finally brings success in creating a butterfly garden or identifying a mystery plant.

For years, readers like you have been sending us tried-and-true secrets for birding and gardening. From attracting hummingbirds and getting rid of bully birds to starting seeds or saving money in the garden, we receive thousands of tips each year.

Now we're bringing some of the best advice to you in this *Birds & Blooms* book, *Birding & Gardening Secrets*. We've organized it by season so it's easy for you to find what you need, and we're including more than 600 ingenious yet simple ideas to help you have your best backyard yet.

Along with the tips, we hope you enjoy the 200+ photos from some of *Birds & Blooms'* best photographers. We worked exclusively with five of our regulars (read more about them on page 190) to make this our most beautiful book ever.

We hope you enjoy this book and learn dozens of secrets to try in your own yard. After all, if it's about who you know, we know some of the best birders and gardeners in North America!

Stacy Tornio

contents

spri
solutions

Indigo bunting

ng

attracting nesters

Blue jay

The secret to attracting lots of nesting birds is offering variety. Plant different kinds of flowers, shrubs and trees, and keep your birdbath sparkling clean.

–AUDREY ANDERSON, *Boyceville, Wisconsin*

When it comes to nest building, each bird species has its own preferences. But birds are masters at improvising with the materials at hand. Readers have reported seeing birds' nests made of these surprising materials.

Bark
Batting
Cellophane
Cotton
Fabric
Feathers
Hair
Leaves
Lichens
Paper money

Petals
Pine needles
Ribbon
Snakeskin
Spanish moss
String
Thistledown
Twigs
Weed stems
Yarn

American robin with nesting material

After I brush my dog,
I save the excess hair for the spring nesting season. I place the fur and short lengths of yarn throughout my yard, then watch birds collect the material for their nests.

–CATHLYN RAMSEY, *Wichita, Kansas*

American goldfinch

Tree swallow

Western bluebird

Here are a few tips to **attract nesting bluebirds** to your yard:

- **The best location for a bluebird house is an area facing or surrounded by open fields,** where the insects they eat and feed to their young are plentiful. Chickadees, on the other hand, prefer houses in a thicket or a stand of small trees and shrubs.
- **Bluebirds appreciate a host of berry trees and shrubs.** Keep two nest boxes near each other—one for bluebirds and the other for tree swallows.
- **Because bluebirds build new nests for each brood, clean out the old one after the young leave.** This encourages a second and third nest in the same house during a single nesting season.

–BERNICE MADDUX, *Weatherford, Texas*

Place an inch of clean cedar shavings in the bottom of birdhouses to provide extra cushioning. Birds incorporate the shavings into their nests.

–BETSY ROGERS, *Puyallup, Washington*

Convert bluebird houses into bed-and-breakfasts by attaching small feeding dishes to the tops of the post for mealworms, commercially produced bluebird food and raisins. The bluebirds can't resist nesting in our yard because of these extra offerings.

–DONALD THALACKER, *Palmyra, Virginia*

These tips on nesting sites and birdhouses provide easy access to your backyard:

Bluebirds love my homemade coffee can birdhouses. I drill a 1 ½-inch hole in the plastic lid and mount the house on a tree through the can's metal bottom. To clean, simply remove the plastic lid.

–SUE MCKEE, *Iuka, Mississippi*

Face bluebird houses east to attract more of these pretty birds. They should be mounted in long open fields.

–MATTHEW YODER, *Bloomfield, Iowa*

Place your nest box in an open field and watch the bluebirds raise their family.

Eastern bluebirds

Birdhouses don't mix with busy roads. I place mine

Since I placed a suet feeder near my bluebird house, lovely eastern varieties have been attracted to the nest box each spring.

–DAVID KENT, *Richmond, Virginia*

Tape the entrances of your bluebird nest boxes shut to keep house sparrows out. Remove the tape once bluebirds arrive.

–JESSE SWAREY, *Belleville, Pennsylvania*

Snakes will avoid bluebird houses if you wrap their mounting posts with aluminum foil.

–SUSIE KING, *Holtwood, Pennsylvania*

Protect your birds' home by placing it in a secluded spot, like an evergreen.

along seldom-traveled roads in our backyard and pasture to prevent unfortunate accidents.

–JOHN KELLER, *Piedmont, Ohio*

I secure nest boxes to trees by wrapping bungee cords around the trunks. It looks nice, holds firmly and doesn't damage the tree the way nails do. Once nesting season is over, I can remove the boxes and store them until next year.

–CLYDE KEELER, *Lanesville, Indiana*

Set up several birdhouses throughout your yard. Be sure to use different-size entrance holes so different species of birds can find a house to use.

–GARY CLARK, *Knowlton, Quebec*

Provide nesting material in a suet cage. This keeps the lightweight material, such as tissue and yarn, from blowing around your backyard.

–GLORIA ASHBAUGH, *Lynchburg, Tennessee*

Carolina wrens are always welcome in my yard—they eat lots of pesky insects. To encourage them to nest here, I place a variety of containers that are about the size of a 1-gallon milk jug around my yard. They've inhabited a swimming pool skimmer, an empty flowerpot, a plastic foam ice chest and an old bookcase. They're not picky when choosing nesting cavities, as long as they're roomy.

–REBECCA KING, *Burlison, Tennessee*

Save quilt trimmings for spring when the birds are collecting nesting material. I leave clusters of the soft yarn throughout my yard. It's a good way to recycle.

–KATHY KERMEN, *Yreka, California*

These pileated woodpeckers make their nest in a tree cavity.

Robins often nest in the woven baskets I mount outside. Simply turn them on their side and attach them to a wall with a few screws. Mount them under an overhang so the birds are protected from the elements.

–CONNIE MOORE, *Medway, Ohio*

Provide mealworms for your bluebirds
in spring. They'll take turns feeding
their young this delicious snack!

Want birds to nest in your birdhouses? *Try these reader-tested tips.*

Watch for nesting activity from your favorite birds.
Once they lay eggs, it's more difficult to find them, so look for birds performing courtship rituals or carrying nesting materials.

–TERI DUNN, *Gloucester, Massachusetts*

Birds prefer to have their houses at different heights.
Purple martin houses must be about 15 to 20 feet above the ground. For bluebirds and tree swallows, post-mount houses about 5 to 8 feet high. House wrens prefer homes that hang 6 to 10 feet above the ground.

Wood is always the best material for birdhouses.
The houses also should have ventilation around the top and drainage holes in the floor, and be painted or stained an earth tone.

To attract more bluebirds,
be sure to space your nest boxes 50 to 100 feet apart.

–TONY SOWERS, *Milo, Iowa*

Pick the proper design.
In addition to specific habitats, different species also require varied types of birdhouses.

Purple martins like to live in communities. Therefore, an apartment-style house or multiple nesting gourds work best. In contrast, house wrens live in small single houses and prefer not to have other wrens close by.

Paint purple martin houses white because it reflects the sun's rays
and keeps the houses cooler. I also place the entrance holes in different locations in each gourd so the martins can determine which house is theirs.

–VICTOR STOLL, *Finger, Tennessee*

We've increased the number of house finches nesting in our yard
by wiring small strawberry baskets in the corners of the awnings on our house. We put up four baskets one year and watched 38 house finches fledge from the nests.

–DORIS BARTEL, *Hillsboro, Kansas*

I've heard that wrens won't nest in a birdhouse if they can see other wrens.
So I'm always careful to place my wren houses out of sight of one another.

–NONA FLEACH, *Belmont, Wisconsin*

Collect fallen branches and make a neat pile for birds.
They not only use the pile of branches for protection, but they also find tiny branches in it for nest building.

–GARY CLARK, *Knowlton, Quebec*

Some birds love our evergreens during nesting season.
The bigger and denser, the better for them to build a nest. Their favorite nesting trees in my yard include our blue spruce tree, Douglas fir and our dwarf Alberta spruce.

–TINA JACOBS, *Wantage, New Jersey*

If you provide pieces of string for birds
during nesting season, remember to cut them into sections only a couple of inches long so birds don't get tangled in them.

–ELEANOR ALFORD, *Chesapeake, Virginia*

seed starting

Feed seedlings half-strength plant food.

Do this every week or so. Proper care will produce plants that are more robust and improve their chances of survival when they move outdoors.

–TERI DUNN, *Gloucester, Massachusetts*

Get your seedlings off to a great start by supplying them with adequate food and water and the correct growing temperature. Find out more on the following pages.

This American robin watches over the newly planted garden from its perch on a plant marker.

Recycled paper egg cartons work well for starting seeds. Cut the top off and place it under the egg compartments. Then fill the compartments with seed-starting mix and seeds. When watered, the paper carton holds moisture and adds support for handling. Break each section apart when transplanting. You can even plant the biodegradable carton with the seedling to reduce any possible transplanting shock.

–GAIL RUSSELL
Greendale, Wisconsin

Plastic berry containers, like the ones you get from the produce section at the grocery store, make great seed starters. The clear cover helps the soil stay moist as the seeds germinate.

–JENNIE TANDY, *Penetang, Ontario*

Use a turkey baster to water plants you have started from seeds indoors. It prevents you from overwatering or flattening the tender plants.

–VALERIE EVANSON
Phoenixville, Pennsylvania

When you start seeds indoors in pots, it's best to plant them in a small amount of dirt first. Gradually add more dirt as the plant grows. Do this and your plants will be much stronger and will do better after you transplant them outside.

–MRS. J.S. MILLHOUSE, *Piqua, Ohio*

I live in a cold climate, so I start my seeds indoors in plastic containers covered with plastic wrap. I place them on my clothes dryer, which heats up the seeds whenever it runs; the seeds germinate in half the time. After the seeds sprout, I move them under grow lights.

—ANGIE COUTURE, *Superior, Wisconsin*

To help my seedlings grow sturdier stems and better prepare them for life outdoors, I connect an automatic timer to a small fan, then aim it at the seedlings. I set the timer to turn the fan on and off every 20 minutes for 12 hours a day.

—GARY SEIDEL, *Pittsburgh, Pennsylvania*

I used to have trouble sowing fine seeds evenly because they're difficult to see—until I learned this simple trick. Mix the tiny seeds with a package of inexpensive gelatin powder, which helps to spread the seeds evenly and lets you easily see where you've sown them.

—KAREN ANN BLAND, *Gove, Kansas*

Before you transplant your
seedlings, give them a chance to
harden off outside.

I grow many of my plants from seed, so I wanted to make a cold frame for the tender seedlings. To save money, I made one from windows donated by friends who had remodeled their homes. Now I can start seeds early with guaranteed success.

–MICHAEL STEELE, *Watkinsville, Georgia*

Use old milk cartons to start seeds. Simply cut off the top of the cardboard carton, punch holes in the bottom and fill with potting mix.

–ARTHUR CHESTER, *Cayce, South Carolina*

If you have mini-blinds that need to be shortened, save the extra slats. I cut them in pieces and use them to mark rows of seeds.

–HELEN SANDERS, *West Union, South Carolina*

My seedlings grow better early in the growing season because I cut the bottoms off 2-liter plastic soft drink bottles and use the tops to protect the tender sprouts. I then use the clear bottoms as saucers for my clay pots. They work well and protect surfaces from spills when I overwater.

–SHIRLEY SALYERS, *Columbus, Ohio*

After spending months babying my new seedlings, I would get discouraged if the sun burned them as they hardened off. So I began covering my young plants during the hottest time of the day with some old pots I had in storage. Once they grew a new set of leaves, they were able to handle the sun on their own, and the pots returned to the basement.

–AMANDA KENNEDY, *Columbia Cross Roads, Pennsylvania*

Foam drinking cups make ideal pots for starting seedlings. They are inexpensive, especially if recycled, and are available in a range of sizes. Just punch a few drainage holes in the bottom of the cups and write plant names on the sides. At planting time, seedlings slip out so easily that I'm able to use the cups many times before discarding them.

–BARBARA HUNT, *Jonesborough, Tennessee*

When I run out of space for seedlings on the basement shelf, which is under lights, I start them in an old aquarium nearby.

–IRENE JONES, *Chardon, Ohio*

Here's an easy way to start seedlings. Fill a cardboard egg carton with potting soil. Use a pencil to make two depressions in each cup—¼ inch deep for small seeds and ½ inch for large ones. Plant two seeds per cup, cover with soil and water lightly. When each plant has four leaves, cut the egg cups apart, remove the cardboard and plant them right in the garden.

–MRS. V. PRINCE, *Houston, Texas*

I use leftover newspaper to make biodegradable planting cups for transplanting seedlings. Cut four thicknesses of newspaper into a 7-inch square, fold it in thirds, then turn and fold again to make a nine-square fold. Angle-fold each corner on one side and staple. Repeat on opposite side.

When seedlings are ready to transplant, plant the entire cup. This won't disturb the seedlings' roots, and the containers will break down on their own.

–PATRICIA MURRAY, *Niles, Ohio*

I use large coffee cans to start most of my seeds indoors, including plants that normally don't withstand transplanting. I cut off the bottom of the can, add drainage slits in the plastic lid, fill it with potting soil and plant my seeds.

After it's warm enough to transfer the seedlings outdoors, I simply remove the plastic lid and slide out the contents—soil and all—to avoid disturbing the tender roots. I've started a lot of plants, including sunflowers, this way.

–LIZ MCCAIN, *Florence, Oregon*

When I start seeds indoors, I cover the containers with disposable shower caps at night to keep the soil moist. The cap's elastic ensures that they fit any shape container.

–PHIL KOZOL, *Glendale Heights, Illinois*

gardening for birds & butterflies

Purple coneflower

Birds love purple coneflower seed heads. Plant a few of the new selections in soft yellow, deep orange and hot pink. As a bonus, they're fragrant, too!

—ELLEN RUOFF RILEY, *Birmingham, Alabama*

American goldfinch

I grow huge sunflowers to feed the birds. I cut off the heads and dry them. When winter comes, I set whole heads in the trees. It's a feast for the birds.

–ROSE KRUSHELNISKI
Nipawin, Saskatchewan

American goldfinches love to feed on false nettle (*Boehmeria*) seeds. Although this plant doesn't have showy flowers, its pretty green leaves make an interesting backdrop for shorter flowering plants.

–MARLENE CONDON
Crozet, Virginia

I plant sunflowers, Mexican sunflowers and zinnias to attract hummingbirds and other beautiful birds. Having plenty of water available for them also helps.

–ELLA LUCAS
Roanoke, Virginia

> *If you grow common milkweed,* you'll be rewarded with the beautiful sight of monarch butterfly caterpillars during summer.
>
> **—MARLENE CONDON,** *Crozet, Virginia*

Monarch on swamp milkweed

Eastern bluebird

I attract eastern bluebirds to my yard with a variety of plantings. Sumac, flowering dogwood, grape, noninvasive honeysuckle, climbing bittersweet, pokeweed and greenbrier seem to be some of their favorite plants.

–ANGELA GRIFFIN HATCHETT, *Altoona, Alabama*

Attract tons of birds by creating a miniature bird haven in an unused corner of your yard. I planted viburnum, ornamental grasses and purple coneflowers. Then I added a shepherd's hook with feeders.

–BARBARA MANHEIM, *New Lenox, Illinois*

I plant wild asters and Mexican sunflowers for the butterflies. When the monarchs start their long trip south, my flowers are covered with them.

–BETTY FUNK, *Iowa City, Iowa*

American painted lady

Include a birdbath in your garden for birds to bathe and get a drink. And what better setting for your photos?

American painted lady

Want more winged wonders in your backyard? Use these handy tips to invite them in.

To entice butterflies and bees to your garden, plant oregano, borage, catnip and hollyhocks.

–ARDITH MORTON, *Merriman, Nebraska*

I plant dill among my flowers to attract mountain swallowtail butterflies. Bouquet and other short varieties of dill blend in easily in my flower beds. I see swallowtails at all different stages of their life cycle each summer.

–JILL WOODS, *Colorado Springs, Colorado*

In my garden, zinnias attract all kinds of butterflies!

–SAMUEL MOTT, *St. Michaels, Maryland*

Marigolds are popular with most butterfly caterpillars, and the seeds are favorites of goldfinches and sparrows. Swallowtail butterflies raise their young on parsley and carrots.

–CAROL SOEHNER, *Centerville, Ohio*

I have touch-me-nots in my garden, and I've noticed hummingbirds and butterflies are attracted to the sweet nectar.

–REBECCA KING, *Burlison, Tennessee*

Butterflies flock to my zinnias and cosmos. Hummingbirds also enjoy the nectar and the insects that are attracted to these blooms.

–P. TAYOR, *Andalusia, Alabama*

The giant black swallowtail butterfly loves parsley.

–LOUISE GRANT, *Fort White, Florida*

Butterflies love containers filled with their favorite plants. Our readers had the most success with attracting butterflies when they followed these simple tips.

- **Create a multilayered effect** with plants at varying heights. Use trailing, bushy and upright varieties to offer nectar at different levels.
- **A flower's color, shape and scent will attract butterflies,** but the biggest draw is the nectar.
- **Include nectar-rich, tubular flowers** as well as plants with daisylike blooms such as purple coneflower, mums, yarrow and butterfly weed.
- **Grow a few containers with host plants** for even more success in attracting butterflies. Use milkweed, mallow or asters in your combinations.

Spotted tiger longwing

Use these plants to attract birds!

Plant trumpet and honeysuckle vines. They will attract hummingbirds and other nectar eaters, like orioles, tanagers, warblers and woodpeckers, to your yard.

–**GEORGIA STEWART**, *Hebron, Illinois*

I design and create patio planters and window boxes containing plants that are highly attractive to birds and butterflies. This allows us to view our flying visitors up close from our patio and porch. Some of my favorite flowers to use in these containers are petunias, phlox, fuchsia, ornamental grasses, zinnias and milkweed.

–**ELLEN SOUSA**, *Spencer, Massachusetts*

Plant mountain ash, honeysuckle, crab apples and a Juneberry tree to attract the birds. By inviting birds to your backyard with these plants, they'll help control the bug population.

–**AZALEA WRIGHT**, *Forest Lake, Minnesota*

I decided to create a "bird island" by placing a birdhouse on either side of a tree. I added a dish feeder and a birdbath near the birdhouses as well.

Once those were in place, I planted petunias, marigolds, daylilies and vincas. Then I put in a few hanging baskets near the birdhouses.

We now have so many birds that enjoy the sanctuary. I never realized how much of a difference it would make to have the birdhouse, feeder and bath together alongside the plants.

–**MARY LOU ROSEMONT**, *Darien, Illinois*

Ruby-throated hummingbird

We attract butterflies with monarda (bee balm) and red carnations.

They also visit my hanging baskets of begonias.

–MARCIA BRIGGS, *Pittsburgh, Pennsylania*

We have dozens of varieties of wildflowers growing on our property. As the plants go to seed, I notice which ones attract the birds. When the wind and rain force the seeds to the ground, I gather them and put them in my feeders. The birds spend less energy by coming to my one-stop-shop café, and I get great exercise collecting the wildflower seeds.

Some of the plants the birds really like are star chickweed, downy rattlesnake plantain and wild sarsaparilla. I try to stick to native plants when growing wildflowers because they grow better and provide the indigenous birds and butterflies with plenty of food.

–BARBARA STANLEY, *Blairsville, Georgia*

The Kentucky blueberry, as it's called here, is the perfect plant for birds. (Its botanical name is *Mahonia*.) This shrub has prickly leaves similar to holly, so it makes a great protective hiding place for songbirds. It also produces fragrant yellow flowers in spring, followed by a smorgasbord of large berries. Eastern bluebirds, American robins, wood thrushes, cedar waxwings, brown thrashers, tufted titmice and northern cardinals flock to my yard to feed on its fruit.

–LISA KIMMICH, *Athens, Georgia*

I've discovered Montana bluets and zinnias provide food for American goldfinches. The birds bend the drying flower heads to the ground as they land on them, then pull out the seeds with their bills. It's fascinating to watch.

–CHARLENE MARGETIAK, *Norwalk, Ohio*

My weigela attracts lots of nectar-feeding birds.

–THERESA MAIORANA, *Ashford, Connecticut*

Pine siskin

Spicebush swallowtail

For more blue jays, try planting plumed cockscomb, marigolds, sunflowers, zinnias, hibiscus and gourds.

–MARSHA MELDER
Shreveport, Louisiana

In spring, plant sunflowers with the birds in mind. At harvesttime, I cut down my sunflowers and remove the seed heads. The I use the leftover stalks to make "tepees" for birds to roost in during cold nights.

It's easy to do. Just gather the tops of the stalks with rope and spread the bottoms for stability. The birds will eat the leftover seeds and will roost in the stalks.

–WILBUR JENSEN
Onalaska, Wisconsin

Daylilies not only fill your yard with dazzling colors, they attract nectar-feeding creatures like hummingbirds and orioles.

–MARLENE CONDON
Crozet, Virginia

Black-capped chickadees can't resist my ponderosa pine. They split open the pinecones and eat the inner seeds.

–ANNE FAUVELL
Rapid City, South Dakota

Keep feathered friends coming to your backyard by planting a mix of trees and shrubs that will produce fruits and berries year-round, not all at the same time.

—EMILY GREY, *Onancock, Virginia*

Birds can't resist the clusters of berries that hang from my viburnum shrub.

—BARBARA MANHEIM, *New Lenox, Illinois*

Rose-breasted grosbeak

garden prep

A full six hours of sunlight a day is essential for good growth and ripening of most vegetables. Morning light is preferable to afternoon because it'll dry dew, which reduces the risk of disease, and is easier on the plants than the afternoon's blazing heat.

–JULIE DRYSDALE, *Aptos, California*

Our spring weather is unpredictable, so I needed a way to control the temperature for my growing vegetables. The answer? I recycled the large plastic bag that held a bedroom comforter. I simply stood it on its side, placed the plants inside and zipped it up.

–CAROL WRIGHT
Johnston, Iowa

Plant several white icicle radish seeds at the base of cucumber and squash seedlings. This discourages insects while providing an extra veggie crop.

–JOYCE BARNHART
Norwalk, Connecticut

Pepper plants have always been a problem for me, but I learned a trick. Once they get a good start inside, I harden them off in boxes in partial sun. Then in spring, I set them in the ground with a plastic milk jug over the top. I pile dirt around the jug to give plants a constant temperature. Once they have grown enough to reach the top of the milk jug, it's safe to remove it. This has worked well for me with all types of peppers!

–PAM KUTZ
Sykeston, North Dakota

Before I plant onions, radishes or carrots,
I sprinkle the row with leaves from a tea bag. I find this keeps root maggots away.

–JOANNE HAMILTON, *Randleman, North Carolina*

Radishes

To make it easier to thin out carrot seedlings, mix carrot and radish seeds in a shaker. Broadcast them in 18-inch-wide strips. As you pick early-maturing radishes, you'll thin out carrot seedlings at the same time.

–SUSAN TATUS MCLARTY, *Oakland County, Michigan*

Before your cucumber vines start to run, put a wire cage over each hill or wire fencing behind each row. The vines climb on the cage or fencing, and cucumbers can't rot on the ground—plus, they're easier to pick!

–LYNWOOD HYLER, *Batesburg, South Carolina*

In the middle of February, I start to save banana peels and store them in a bag in the freezer. When it's time to plant tomatoes, I dig a ditch 2 inches deeper than required, lay the peels end to end and cover them with dirt. Then I plant the tomatoes as usual. My tomato vines reached 8 to 10 feet, and the fruits were very sweet.

–KATHY MAULLER, *Manchester, Missouri*

No room for a garden? That doesn't mean you can't grow vegetables. We grow ours in containers on the driveway. We grow tomatoes, peppers, green onions, peas and pole beans.

–ELLEN AND ROGER CAYWOOD
Olympia, Washington

Plant two veggies in one pot. I tried planting leaf lettuce around the edges of a big pot with carrots in the middle. Both did very well.

–MARY MARGARET COSENS
Mackinaw City, Michigan

Plan ahead for a **healthy garden in spring**

A child's plastic sled works just as well as an expensive garden cart for transporting flats of plants, heavy bags of soil, pots and other items from the shed or garage out to the garden.

–RITA CHRISTIANSON, *Glenburn, North Dakota*

Use an extra calendar—or an old calendar—to remind yourself when to do various garden chores. Each time you learn about new planting or care instructions, write the information under the appropriate date.

For example, I remind myself to prune grapes on Feb. 22, repot and fertilize poinsettias on May 1 and plant spring bulbs on Oct. 15. It doesn't matter what year the calendar is. This just lets me know the time of year each job should be done.

After several years of adding information, my calendar is fairly complete, and I can tell at a glance what chores need to be done each month. As a result of my planning, my yard has never looked better!

–JENNIE TANDY, *Penetang, Ontario*

In early spring, we punch holes in the bottom of a large can and use it to sprinkle hardwood ashes over the snow in the garden. The snow melts quickly and the earth dries out faster, enabling us to plant earlier. But if you have alkaline soil, use the ashes sparingly.

–GERRI KUREC, *Cambridge, Ontario*

VEGETABLE DISPLAY, TERRY WILD STOCK

Die-hard gardeners will tell you that a garden is a work in progress. But if you thoughtfully plan before you plant, your landscape will beautifully endure for years to come without costly and time-consuming alterations or additions.

1 Look at the big picture. Sketch out an overall picture of your yard, including entertaining areas, your house and other buildings. Enlarge the sketch and mark off existing landscape features like trees, shrubs and gardens. Pencil in proposed plantings to see how they fit in the existing landscape.

2 Create a budget. Determine how much you want to spend for this year's plantings, mulch and soil amendments. Plan on putting in paths and buying the larger structural plants first. When the budget is tight, think about filling in your design over the course of several years.

3 Consider every season. Slot in plants with different bloom times to ensure a succession of blossoms throughout the year.

–TERI DUNN, *Gloucester, Massachusetts*

4 Pick a palette. Are you partial to pastels? Do red-hot hues get your creative juices flowing? Working within a color scheme will help you set a cohesive scene and prevent you from buying unsuitable plants during weaker moments.

Here's an easy way to help identify what type of soil you have. Place a cup of garden dirt in a clear quart jar and fill the jar with water until it is well mixed. Then let it settle for 24 hours.

The elements in the soil will separate into layers. The layer with the heaviest particles—sand—will be on the bottom, followed by layers of silt and clay.

You should be able to estimate the amount of sand, silt and clay in your soil by the thickness of each layer.

–ANGELA GRIFFIN HATCHETT, *Altoona, Alabama*

Transforming your yard will seem less overwhelming if you do it in sections. Each summer since we've been living in our new house, we've chosen a different area to landscape.

–JOHN DUNZELMAN, *Barnegat, New Jersey*

Planting flowers according to their height (tallest in back and shortest in front) helps prevent them from falling over. For example, plant tall cannas in the rear of the flower bed, then shorter cosmos in front of them, then gladioli and finally marigolds as border plants.

–MONICA BENGSTON, *Independence, Iowa*

A planting schedule change at the start of the season can make a major difference for a continuous harvest. Instead of planting everything at once, stagger your start days. This can be as simple as planting half your vegetables around Memorial Day and a second round a week or two later. Or plant a row a week over a period of four or five weeks. This works beautifully to supply you with a longer harvest.

–BOB HANNA, *Leominster, Massachusetts*

feeding spring birds

Baltimore oriole

Orioles and tanagers will come to backyards for orange halves. And if you can buy them in season, they're a budget-friendly choice! Orioles will also stop by for grapes.

To attract orioles to your yard, plant nectar-producing flowers like red-hot poker, as well as flowering and fruit-bearing trees and shrubs.

–ALLISON SCHOTT
Brantford, Ontario

One spring, I could hear the Baltimore orioles singing, but they wouldn't come near my feeding area. I tried putting orange halves in the trees, but the birds came only occasionally and wouldn't stay.

Finally, I came up with a solution. I made holes in the bottoms of the orange halves and fitted them right over the rod loops of my feeder. The orioles found these right away, and I loved seeing them so close to my house.

The trick to bringing the birds back is to put a fresh orange out every morning. You can't leave an old one out there or they'll lose interest and go someplace else. Good luck!

–JULIE A. CHRISTIANSEN
Charlevoix, Michigan

Azaleas

Here are a few tips to attract spring birds:

My husband suspended a muffin tin from wires to make an oriole feeder. The lip of the tin serves as a perch, and the cups hold orange halves and sugar water, which they love.

–**MARCY CELLA**, *L'Anse, Michigan*

I hang a suet cage at the edge of our yard and attach orange slices to it in spring. This not only attracts suet-eating birds, but also brings in beautiful Baltimore orioles.

–**DIANE GRATTON**, *Knowlton, Quebec*

I've discovered a great oriole food that can be served in a sugar-water feeder. Simply mix ⅓ quart grape jelly with 3 cups water and blend well. The orioles can't get enough of this fruity nectar.

–**MARIANNE BUDAHN**, *Darwin, Minnesota*

Scatter raisins around your yard immediately after spotting your first American robin in spring. Because they'll often arrive when the ground is still frozen, it's hard for them to find worms. So they really make use of this offering.

–**RUTH WOLTRING**, *Grafton, Wisconsin*

When worms are scarce in early spring, I leave pieces of suet on the ground for the American robins. They feed on it until the weather warms.

–**PHYLLIS SCHABACKER**, *Fountain City, Wisconsin*

I discovered a terrific springtime meal for young birds. I set out a few slices of raw potato, and a mother bird stopped by to feed her fledglings pieces of it.

–**LILLIAN WILLIAMS**, *Houston, Texas*

To feed American goldfinches, I use a large cheesecloth bag and fill it with thistle seed. I hang it from a wire fence in my backyard and watch the finches flock to it.

–**MARGUERITE DEBNAM**, *Greensboro, North Carolina*

I supply grape jelly in large quantities. My oriole feeder has a protective roof and a deep plastic dish for holding heaping servings of jelly.

–**ROLAND JORDAHL**, *Pelican Rapids, Minnesota*

We love to attract orioles in spring and then watch them all summer long. We wanted a feeder that would attract as many of them as possible, so I came up with a plan.

First I took two orange plastic bowls. Then I put a ½-inch-thick piece of round plywood inside, with a 3-inch hole to accommodate a cup for holding jelly. I added three dowels to hold the top and bottom together. The orioles lock their long toes around these spindles to balance while they're eating.

I devised the entire thing to look like an orange. It works, because the orioles stick around my yard all summer.

–RAY WIGERN, *Blue Earth, Minnesota*

This nectar recipe is irresistible to hummingbirds and orioles. Prepare the basic sugar-water mix (4 cups water to 1 cup sugar, boil and cool), then add this special ingredient—a couple of drops of orange extract. The birds will flock to it.

–ANNA FRIE, *Burtrum, Minnesota*

Baltimore oriole

Here's how to
attract
more orioles

I was looking for an easy way to make a Baltimore oriole feeder using things I found around the house. I took several pieces of hardware cloth and wire to make a holder for a shot glass, which we fill with grape jelly. The orioles love it, and house finches have eaten from it, too.

–ARDITH BRANAN, *Clarinda, Iowa*

Make sure your feeder has large enough perches and drinking ports. It's not unusual for orioles to try hummingbird feeders, but their bills are often too big.

–ANNE SCHMAUSS, *Santa Fe, New Mexico*

I've discovered that strawberry preserves

A week before orioles are due back to our area, I place small tuna cans filled with grape jelly on our deck rails.

—BEV KALSEM, *Madrid, Iowa*

You don't need a special feeder to invite orioles to your yard this spring. Just take an old suet cage feeder and fill it with oranges instead. The orioles will love this special treat!

I've discovered that orioles prefer the cheaper generic brands of grape jelly to the more expensive name brands.

—COLLEEN JOHNSON, *Monticello, Minnesota*

are a great way to attract orioles. I smear some on toast, and they love it!

—DONNA JABLONSKI, *Kulpmont, Pennsylvania*

Eastern bluebird

Western bluebird

I experimented with a wild birdseed blend that included dried cherries. Bluebirds don't normally eat cherries, so I took a closer look to see if they'd eat the mix.

Turns out they were plucking the cherries from the mixture. Now I always throw a couple of handfuls of dried cherries or raisins into the seed when I refill the feeder.

–MRS. DALLAS WALKER, *Milan, Georgia*

Aside from mealworms, we've found that the bluebirds in our yard also like this creation we like to call Miracle Meal. Here's the recipe:

1 cup lard or beef suet

1 teaspoon corn oil

4 cups yellow cornmeal

1 cup all-purpose flour

Melt the lard or suet and then stir in the other ingredients. Add anything else you think the bluebirds might like, including raisins and sunflower hearts.

After the mixture sets, cut it into chunks and serve as suet. To make the bluebirds really happy, try adding some mealworms as well. We offer this Miracle Meal every morning and evening, and the bluebirds always come back for more.

–EVA EVERY, *Elsie, Michigan*

To help bluebirds get accustomed to my enclosed mealworm feeder, I prop open the hinged top with a stick. After they've come into the box a few times through its side entrances, I remove the stick. Once they've found this source of mealworms, they'll keep coming back for more.

–PATTI FARNUM, *Nashville, Michigan*

Buy wax worms or mealworms from a local bait shop and set a few on a tray feeder. The bluebird parents will snatch them up and take them to their chicks.

–JERILYN VELTUS, *Neillsville, Wisconsin*

Bluebirds love cooked grits. I leave a batch out every morning before nesting season to entice them to my backyard.

–CHARLOTTE HEINZE, *Davie, Florida*

Eastern bluebird

We feed finches all year long, so there are always a lot of them around. Instead of using tube feeders, which only feed six to 12 finches at a time, we have figured out our own system.

We buy a few yards of cheap, loosely woven burlap from the fabric store and use it to make several 6-by-10-inch bags. We fill the bags with nyjer seed and then hang them from rope. The finches make their own small holes to get at the seed, and a single bag can feed as many birds as two of our old feeders.

–FRED KAMP, *Rittman, Ohio*

American goldfinch

I use a watering can to make filling my feeders a breeze. Just remove the head from the spout and pour your mixture in. It's perfect for filling small feeders.

–**CARL CORRELL**, *Munfordville, Kentucky*

I attach terra-cotta flowerpot saucers to posts around my deck and fill them with birdseed. It's an inexpensive way to serve all of my feathered friends.

–**SHERYL NEAL**, *Carrollton, Ohio*

I saw American goldfinches everywhere, but they never visited my feeders. One day, my co-worker offered me an old yellow bird feeder. I cleaned it up, and in less than 10 minutes I had goldfinches fighting for a port at the feeder.

Now I recommend this to everyone struggling to attract goldfinches. I don't know whether it's a coincidence, but if you're trying to attract goldfinches, it might be worth it to add a yellow feeder to your yard.

–**CINDIE MEAD**, *Correctionville, Iowa*

It's easy to attract northern cardinals to your backyard. To keep them happy year-round, set out black-oil sunflower seeds, their favorite food. And for even more traffic, install a birdbath. When spring comes, you'll have plenty of cardinals flying around.

–**ROBERT GREENE**, *Acworth, Georgia*

With young children, there often are leftover peanut butter and jelly sandwiches after lunch. So we give the extras to the birds. We just place the pieces on a tray feeder and watch the birds finish the meal.

–**ELAINE SCHMIT**, *Mt. Pleasant Mills, Pennsylvania*

We had several bird feeders in our yard, but not many winged visitors. Since there were no trees in the immediate area, we placed a wooden rack used to dry clothes nearby. I figured it would serve as a kind of protective cover and a spot for birds to perch as they checked out the surroundings before landing on the feeder. As soon as we did this, we noticed more birds.

–**LESLIE DEMARGERIE**, *Sprague, Manitoba*

The orioles were driving the hummingbirds from their feeders, so I started putting out grape jelly to distract them. I set out jar lids filled with the stuff. In a matter of minutes, the orioles migrated to the jelly-filled lids, much to the delight of the hummingbirds.

To make the lids more secure, I nail them to the top of a fence post or attach them to the porch railing with double-sided tape.

–**COLENE CHEBUHAR**, *Des Moines, Iowa*

Cooked spaghetti looks a lot like mealworms, which is why I think my backyard birds love it. I cook up about a cup of the pasta, then add a little peanut butter and bacon grease to it before cutting it into 1-inch pieces and setting it out for the birds.

–**PAT STARK**, *Nevada, Missouri*

summ

solutions

mer

American goldfinch

container savings

Hens-and-chicks

This old instrument makes a picturesque place to plant impatiens. What do you have that can be converted?

Just about anything can be recycled into a planter. Line a basket with plastic (but keep it under cover from rain), or fill old cowboy boots with gravel, potting soil and plants. Impatiens and ivy look especially good spilling over the tops of boots.

–CHRISTINE OLSON, *Seiad Valley, California*

Filling large flowerpots with soil can get expensive. To avoid this, I put empty aluminum cans in the bottom of the pot. This keeps my pots much lighter, and I still have really gorgeous flowers.

–VI CONCANNON, *Fair Oaks, California*

I wanted more containers for my garden, but I needed a budget-friendly idea. So I transformed old plastic containers from the garden center. All I did was take some burlap and wrap the containers with it. Then I used pieces of twine to hold it in place. The burlap gives the containers an earthy look.

–COLLEEN HATTLER, *East Aurora, New York*

Plant stands don't have to be expensive. Last year I used a stepladder as a stand for my flower containers. It's been a great way to display my marigolds and other annuals.

–FRANCES MOORE, *Burgessville, Ontario*

When I plant containers, I always place a used dryer sheet at the bottom of my pots. This way, no potting soil falls through the holes, and I can still water my plants properly since the dryer sheet allows for good drainage.

–DONNA MOON, *Woodgate, New York*

I bought plastic laundry tubs for $7 each and drilled holes in the bottom for drainage. Then I removed the rope handles and painted them with colorful flowers. I now have great decorative containers, and they were a fraction of the cost of similar ones.

–BOBBI CHILDERS, *Perry, Florida*

Fill an old wheelbarrow with potting soil and plants, then place it wherever you need a point of interest or color.

–GAY NICHOLAS, *Henderson, Texas*

Use 5-gallon buckets inside large ceramic decorator pots that don't have drain holes. Drill holes in the bottoms of the buckets for drainage and place them on top of large rocks or bricks inside the pot.

–REIS POND, *Thousand Oaks, California*

I'm careful about how much water my containers get. Sometimes I'll water early in the morning and late in the evening if it's been especially hot and windy. And I hand-water everything so I can control the amount my lawn and plants receive. This gets me great results.

–SUNNIE GREENWALT, *Melrose, New Mexico*

My neighbors were throwing out their wooden garage door, so I asked if I could use it as a container for my herb garden. All I needed to make it into the planter of my dreams were nails and paint—which I bought for under $5.

–DEBRA SCHWAB, *Dousman, Wisconsin*

Containers can go anywhere, from this fence post (above) to a tipped-over barrel (right).

Love to save money? Try these DIY container tips and **don't spend a penny!**

When I discovered a dead tree in our yard, my husband cut it down and divided it into several pieces with a chain saw. Then we hollowed the pieces out and added a little soil. Now these old logs make great containers for my impatiens. Since they come from nature, they're absolutely free!

–ALMA DEUTSCH, *Raymore, Saskatchewan*

It's easy to make inexpensive planters with cinder blocks. One or two make a simple, small planter, while a row makes an attractive border. They can be stacked and grouped in any number of configurations. Just fill them with potting soil and plant away for an instant container solution.

–MARY ANN GOVE, *Cottonwood, Arizona*

I had pavers left over from a small patio project, so I stacked and staggered them as a flowerpot stand. It was an attractive way to use old patio bricks.

–MACK ORDUBEGIAN, *St. Catharines, Ontario*

We line large pots with layers of old newspaper before adding soil and plants. This helps keep the pots from drying out so fast. In addition, we use less water and the roots don't "cook" on hot days. When we use this method with potted tomato plants, they last well into fall.

–LUCY LONDON, *Florence, Oregon*

Whenever I repot container plants, I put six or seven pieces of activated charcoal in the bottom of each new pot. The charcoal absorbs excess water, which makes it very difficult to overwater my plants.

–CANDIE CARTE, *Burkesville, Kentucky*

When choosing pots for planting vegetables outdoors, bigger is definitely better, in my opinion. The plants thrive because the soil doesn't dry out as fast.

–ELLEN GAUGLER, *Hoselaw, Alberta*

One of the best flowers to use in containers is impatiens. They thrive anywhere. I planted some in a large circular container, where they grew more than 4 feet tall!

–DEE JAYNE, *Johnston, Iowa*

Use an inexpensive plastic birdbath to add colorful flowers to a shady spot. Make a few holes in the basin for drainage and add potting soil. Then fill with plants that do well in shade and spill over the sides.

–EVELYN IDEN, *Filion, Michigan*

For an interesting planter, fill an old pair of work boots or an old lunch box with soil. Don't forget to make drain holes.

–DARLENE WYNESS, *Williams Lake, British Columbia*

To provide a sweep of color on our small lot, we use several different types of planters together. We put low ones in front, with taller planters and hanging baskets rising toward our fence top. This gives the impression that we have acres of flowers spilling beyond our patio fence.

–JOSEPH AND MARY STEMACH, *Eureka, California*

An old grain seeder used as a planter

This old butter churn makes a great planter when turned on its side. It's the perfect rustic addition to the garden.

Pumpkins make bright autumn planters. I just cut off the tops, scrape out the seeds and fibers and add pots of chrysanthemums. I also use them as vases for fresh-cut flowers. Just add water!

–EDITH GOWEN, *Westbrook, Maine*

You won't have to water plants as often if you use water-retaining crystals. They store moisture and slowly release it as the plants need it. When I buy a plant, I mix the crystals into the soil of a larger container and repot the plant. I've had a lot of success with this method.

–MARY MOORE RITCHIE, *Raleigh, North Carolina*

This old sled was turned into a plant stand for impatiens.

You never know what might make a great container. Shop your local Goodwill or thrift store to find hidden treasures.

hummingbird tips

Female ruby-throated
hummingbird at cardinal flower

I hang my hummingbird feeder in a shady area about 5 feet from the ground. The nectar stays fresh longer in the shade, and the height makes it easy for me to take the feeder down when it needs cleaning.

–ALICE NELSON, *Beloit, Wisconsin*

Hang a hummingbird feeder from the same hook as a hanging basket of impatiens. You'll be giving the hummingbirds a double treat.

–CYNTHIA HILTON, *Nobleboro, Maine*

Provide several sugar-water feeders for hummingbirds, but make sure they're out of sight of one another. The males don't like to share.

–ROBERTA MISTRETTA, *Tucker, Georgia*

Male ruby-throated

Tall, nectar-producing plants are the trick

when it comes to attracting hummingbirds. My cannas seem to be one of their favorite flowers to feed from.

–BARBARA MOHR, *Elkhorn, Wisconsin*

Juvenile ruby-throated at butterfly bush

Hummingbirds use dandelion seeds to line their nests, so I let these weeds go in my backyard. When it comes to nectar, I've discovered they love Mexican sunflowers, marigolds, periwinkle, lantana, cosmos, morning glories and impatiens.

–LOUISE GRANT, *Fort White, Florida*

I attract hummingbirds by setting out pieces of cantaloupe and other melons. Not only do the hummers like the juicy fruit, but fruit flies are also attracted to it, giving the birds even more to eat.

–DEREK ALBRECHT, *St. Cloud, Minnesota*

I could never get my hummingbird feeders completely clean until I discovered this method. Place a few uncooked navy beans in the feeder with some water, and then gently shake. Even the hard-to-reach crevices come clean.

–LYNN RAY, *Greenup, Illinois*

Hollyhocks

Hummingbirds used to fight for spots at my sugar-water feeders until they drove each other out of my yard completely. So I took down my feeders and concentrated on planting red flowers. Now the birds have returned and peacefully feed on nectar from my pentas, hibiscus and roses.

–LAURA OAKES, *Eustis, Florida*

Hummingbirds don't like to wait for their food while I wash their sugar-water feeder, so I hang a spare one while I'm busy cleaning.

–JUDY TALBOTT, *Rochester, Indiana*

An old toothbrush is my secret weapon for cleaning sugar-water feeders. It's great for getting into the small feeding ports.

–MRS. DAVID ROSS, *Henderson, Tennessee*

I attach a handheld watering wand to a trellis that's covered with trumpet vine. The hummingbirds can't resist zipping through the shower of water.

–GLORIA MEREDITH, *Harrington, Delaware*

Leave hummingbird feeders filled with fresh nectar for a few weeks after most hummers have left for the winter. Hummingbirds passing through will welcome the favor.

–CONNIE GARLAND, *Greenwood, Indiana*

I haven't seen a single plant attract more hummingbirds than our potted Million Bells calibrachoa. By adding a sugar-water feeder, we've made the perfect hummingbird haven. They keep coming back for more.

–SHARON BOHDAN, *Greenfield, Wisconsin*

I plant peas on trellises between my nectar feeders. This seems to deter hummingbirds from claiming the feeders as their own and bullying others, because it helps prevent visual contact between the birds. And the pea blossoms provide an additional source of nectar.

–JIM LOW, *Jefferson City, Missouri*

I found that just about anything red that holds water will work as a hummingbird feeder. When I was in a pinch one spring, I used a red soup ladle filled with sugar water. I just fastened it to a porch post with electrical tape and watched the winged wonders feed.

–PHYLLIS MEYER, *Franklin Springs, New York*

My children and I learned that if we rest our fingers on the perches of our hummingbird feeders, the birds will readily perch on them as they drink the sugar water. The experience is amazing!

–DEBBIE EBERTING, *Clinton, Missouri*

I carry a small hummingbird feeder and instant nectar with me when traveling in the summer. That way, I can easily check out the hummingbird traffic in other states. It's fun to see who will come flying along to visit my cottage deck or hotel window.

–DEANNA FRAUTSCHI, *Bloomington, Illinois*

I've found that glass hummingbird feeders are easier to clean and stay clean longer. The hummers never have to wait for their nectar because I have a clean feeder waiting in the wings to replace the one that needs scrubbing.

–BILLIE DAVIS, *Lake Havasu City, Arizona*

Hang red ribbons or a red hand towel near your hummingbird feeders to attract attention. Once the birds see red, they'll find your feeder in a hurry.

–TINA JACOBS, *Wantage, New Jersey*

I place red artificial flowers directly below my hummingbird feeders. The birds might not notice the sugar water at first, but once they realize the blooms are fake, it doesn't take long for them to investigate the feeders.

–CAROL WOODLAND, *Annapolis Royal, Nova Scotia*

Hummingbirds sometimes fly into my garage and get stuck. To help them out, I just place a pot of bright-red flowers in the doorway. This method hasn't failed yet!

–GEORGIA DUMMERS, *Winfield, West Virginia*

Hang wire coat hangers near sugar-water feeders. The hummingbirds perch on the hangers to wait their turn at the feeder, and sometimes you can even watch them preen themselves there.

–KAREN LAABS, *Spokane, Washington*

We plant lots of pink chenille near our sugar-water feeders, as well as amaryllis, bee balm, oriental lilies and hibiscus. Hummingbirds love this assortment, which we have also planted throughout our yard.

–BECCA BRASFIELD, *Burns, Tennessee*

Although hummingbirds aren't often seen in our area, I was able to attract them with a little patience. I diligently changed the sugar water in my feeder every few days and planted lots of red tubular flowers, like petunias, nearby. I was lucky to host a male and several female ruby-throated hummingbirds throughout the summer.

–PHYLLIS SCHANTZ, *Cherry Hill, New Jersey*

Feeding hummingbirds

used to be a chore, but here are some shortcuts I've learned over the years that have made it easier:

- **Homemade nectar**—When you make a sugar-water solution (4 parts water to 1 part sugar, boil and cool), make a large batch. After the solution cools completely, measure how much liquid is needed to fill your feeder and pour equal amounts into resealable freezer bags.

  As I need a refill, I simply remove a bag from the freezer and thaw it on the counter or in the microwave. Then just pour it into the feeder.

- **Cleaning**—Sometimes black mold forms inside my hummingbird feeders. To clean them, I simply break up a denture-cleaning tablet and add it to the reservoir with plain water. It works great.

  After the tablet does its work, I thoroughly rinse the feeder. If stubborn stains remain, add a tablespoon of salt to plain water in the feeder and shake vigorously. The grains of salt will scrub the reservoir. I like these methods because they're nontoxic.

- **Pesky ants**—Here in Texas, fire ants are a terrible problem. They raid and clog my feeders so hummingbirds can't feed.

  Again, I've discovered a simple nontoxic remedy. I spray the feeder's hanger with a light coating of nonstick cooking spray. Ants don't like this spray, but it doesn't seem to bother the hummingbirds.

  –**WALTER NORVELL**, *Fort Worth, Texas*

Female ruby-throated

Ruby-throated hummingbird

A mixture of hanging baskets and sugar-water feeders is heaven for hummers.

Wasps are pests at hummingbird feeders. I've resolved the problem with cooking oil. Each time I clean out my feeder, I dip my finger in oil and rub it around the feeding ports. No more wasps.

–BETTY ROCHESTER
Pine Bluff, Arkansas

In summer, I have to fill my large hummingbird feeders daily in order to keep up with the big appetites of these petite birds. That means boiling up a lot of sugar water for our visitors. In order to cut down on the work and leave room in the refrigerator for our food, I now make a syrup with a 1-to1 ratio of water and sugar. When I fill the feeders, I simply mix a cup of the syrup with 3 cups of water. It's very handy.

–CAROLE MILLER
Meeker, Colorado

Hummingbirds seem to enjoy my sugar-water feeders more since I attached a plastic coffee can lid to the bottom of the feeders using epoxy. The lid serves as a perch, allowing the tiny birds to rest as they eat.

–KLAUS BANDLE
Malden, Massachusetts

*We have a small pond in our backyard
with a waterfall that produces a light mist.*
The hummingbirds love to whiz through the mist and drink from the pond.

–HELEN MILLER, *Evant, Texas*

Juvenile ruby-throated at bee balm

While hummingbirds are attracted to red flowers, there's no need to use red food coloring in homemade sugar water. A clear solution of 4 parts water to 1 part sugar works just fine—there's plenty of red on the outside of commercial feeders to attract the birds.

Don't forget to boil the solution for about a minute and let it cool before serving. Change the sugar water every three to five days so that it doesn't ferment, and keep leftovers in the refrigerator for up to a week.

–GARY CLARK, *Knowlton, Quebec*

For a hummingbird-friendly yard, plant lots of penta flowers near your sugar-water feeders.

–DORIS ALLEN, *Houston, Texas*

I prefer attracting hummingbirds with nectar-producing plants rather than messing with homemade sugar-water solutions.

One of their favorite plants is fuchsia, which hangs near our patio. It gives us a chance to get a close look at these fascinating creatures.

In July, our hostas, red salvia and lavender begin to bloom, providing visitors with even more nectar.

–MRS. GLEN LAMBRIGHT, *Topeka, Indiana*

It's important to keep hummingbird feeders clean and filled with fresh sugar water. The sweet solution quickly spoils in warm weather. I wash my feeders with hot water and refill them every two to three days.

–ALICE PFISTER, *Simi Valley, California*

Black-chinned on penstemon

Female ruby-throated with nestlings

A juvenile ruby-throated and monarch both go after the same treat of butterfly bush.

While my yard blooms with dozens of red, pink and orange tubular flowers that hummingbirds love, I've found that some of their favorites are red columbine, coral bells, Canterbury bells, cardinal flowers, fuchsia, hollyhocks, impatiens, phlox and red salvia.

–GLORIA MEREDITH, *Harrington, Delaware*

veggie care

When you prune the side branches off your tomato plants, save them to plant in your garden. The cuttings will root easily. And when your first tomato plants are finished producing, the cuttings will carry on where they left off.

—**MARSHA MELDER**, *Shreveport, Louisiana*

When my green pepper plants begin to blossom, I put several drops of honey on each plant. This attracts bees, which pollinate the plants. I repeat this several times as the peppers blossom, and I grow the biggest and best peppers in the neighborhood.

—**RUTH GRIFFIN**, *Randolph, New York*

I don't plant green beans until I've harvested all my peas. I pull up the pea vines, till that row, then plant the beans, generally around July 1. I harvest three times more beans this way, because the peas add nitrogen to the soil.

—**VIRGIL DOWNS**, *Mansfield, Ohio*

Early blight can cause tomatoes' lower leaves to develop spots, turn brown and drop, leaving fruit with no protection from sunscald. The blight is caused by fungus spores in the soil splashing onto leaves. Keep this disease to a minimum by mulching, watering only at the plants' bases and pruning out the leaves 5 to 6 inches from the ground.

—**SHARON FOUTCH**, *Letts, Iowa*

Plant your veggies and **watch them grow!**

Rather than blanch leek stalks with soil, I use marsh hay. This keeps them much cleaner and saves a lot of time washing them after harvest.

—SUE GRONHOLZ

Columbus, Wisconsin

Planting a marigold between tomato plants helps keep aphids and other insects away. I rarely have needed to use insecticide.

—JAMES BURTON

Mount Juliet, Tennessee

Pick vegetables frequently. Some plants, including

After your peas stop producing, cut them down with the lawn mower. Water several times and watch them start to produce again.

—GEORGE AND SARAH BAKER
Winnsboro, Texas

Don't throw old sheer curtains away. They're perfect for covering cabbage plants to keep destructive moths from laying eggs there. They're also a good cover for lettuce in hot weather.

—LIZZIE ANN SCHWARTZ
Mount Perry, Ohio

Tripods used for floral and cemetery displays make ideal supports for peppers, eggplants and tall flowers. Place a tripod over a pepper plant when it's small and tie the stems to the supports with panty hose.

—DIANE COVINGTON
Winterville, Georgia

summer squash, cucumbers and peppers, will stop producing if you let them mature or go to seed.

—BETTY BROCKBANK, *Ojai, California*

Beans growing on a trellis

Beets

Cucumber and pickles

Leeks

My method for growing cucumbers produces a prolific crop in record time. Last year I planted six hills on May 15. I picked my first cucumber a little more than a month later, on June 24. And the bounty continued throughout summer. I stopped counting the harvest when I got to 700!

My secret for quick maturation and extended productivity is feeding and watering through a tube. I put a 12-inch section of 4-inch pipe in the center of each hill and plant five seedlings around it.

To water, I fill the pipe to overflowing every other day. Once a week, I mix in a dose of vegetable or flowering plant fertilizer and fill the pipe again.

This slow-watering method encourages the plants' roots to grow deep. I've raised cucumbers this way for 10 years and have never harvested fewer than 450 in a season.

I've found the technique works on other vine plants as well. Give it a try with pumpkins, zucchini, squash and melons.

—KEN SOHL, *Richmond Heights, Ohio*

I grow tomatoes in a raised bed in the city. By the time the tomatoes had barely turned pink, the squirrels were devouring them. My solution? Slip sandwich bags over the ripening tomatoes and seal each bag near the stem. The squirrels don't touch them, and I can even reuse the bags.

—JEAN WILLIAMS, *Stillwater, Oklahoma*

When harvesting broccoli heads, cut the stalks at an angle to prevent the remaining stalk from filling with water and decomposing. The side shoots can then produce better broccoli.

—DEBORAH MOYER, *Liberty, Pennsylvania*

Tomatoes are heavy feeders, so provide them with plenty of compost. Water deeply at ground level, never from the top.

—MARJORIE CAREY, *Freeport, Florida*

At the end of the season, wrap leftover green tomatoes in newspaper and put them in a cool spot. When you want to use them, bring them out of storage, unwrap them and let them ripen in your kitchen.

—JIM BAILY JR., *Long Beach, California*

For an impressive crop of potatoes, try this: Place a tire on the ground, fill it with potting soil and plant a few potatoes. When they begin to sprout, place another tire on top of the first one, filling it with more soil.

Each time you see more potato sprouts, add another tire. When it's time to harvest, remove the tires. A tall tire stack means a great yield of potatoes.

—CHRIS HALE, *Avilla, Indiana*

When my potted tomato plant started to die, a neighbor told me to put a tea bag in the pot, cover it with a little dirt and add water. To my amazement, the plant was green and growing again within a few days!

—MILDRED BRITTON, *Glendale, California*

To boost production of green pepper plants, I sprinkle them with an Epsom salts solution soon after planting. Mix 3 to 4 tablespoons in a gallon of water. Continue sprinkling until the peppers set.

—MARILYN BRUSVEN, *Montevideo, Minnesota*

Leave parsnips in the ground until after the first hard frost. They'll be much sweeter.

—PATRICIA MURRAY, *Niles, Ohio*

summer birding

American goldfinch

Tufted titmouse

To attract American goldfinches and dark-eyed juncos, I make several bouquets of dried flowers and hang them from tree branches. Sunflowers, coneflowers, black-eyed Susans and others that produce seeds are perfect for these bouquets, and late summer is a good time to collect them.

–MARLA BENCH, *Vancouver, Washington*

Birdbaths are one of the best-kept secrets of the garden...

During a heat wave last year, I noticed that the water in my birdbath was extremely hot. I came up with an easy solution to combat the heat: I filled a cottage cheese container with water and froze it overnight. The next morning, I placed it in the middle of the birdbath. This kept the water cool for hours.

–BERNADINE PAWELEK, *Peterborough, Ontario*

I purchased a grill brush to keep my birdbath looking clean. Its wire bristles are strong enough to break up the most stubborn grime.

–BARBARA SIMPSON, *Blue Mountain, Mississippi*

Here's an easy way to make your birdbath sparkle. Toss a handful of sand into the basin and scrub it with a clean brush. The grit helps grind away residue.

–MARILYN CLANCY, *Englewood, Florida*

My birdbaths get cleaned at night while I sleep. I fill the basins with water and add 2 ounces of household bleach. Then I cover them with trash can lids to keep critters out. In the morning, I remove the lids, thoroughly rinse the baths and refill with water.

–EARL RATZ, *Stratford, Ontario*

Don't throw away used pieces of heavy-duty aluminum foil. Crumple them to use as birdbath scrubbers. They work like scouring pads and don't cost a thing. I've found that old mesh onion bags work well, too.

–LOIS NIETERT, *McMurray, Pennsylvania*

Last year we put a new plant near our birdbath, and placed a tomato cage over the plant to encourage upright growth. Even though the plant didn't survive, the cage still stands. The birds love to perch on it, often preening themselves there after their bath.

–STEVEN LENART, *St. Clair Beach, Ontario*

When it's time to wash my birdbath, I just use items I have lying around the house. I simply empty the water, pour baking soda into the basin and scrub it with a paper towel. I've found this method cleans even the dirtiest baths.

–MICHELLE LOOMIS, *Oswego, New York*

Instead of buying a fountain, hang a hose from a tree limb above your birdbath. The birds will be attracted to the sound.

–JOAN ALLEN, *Aiken, South Carolina*

When summer's heat quickly evaporates the water in my birdbaths, I set out a child's rigid plastic wading pool, fill the bottom with sand and rocks, set a couple of water-tolerant plants in it and fill it with a few inches of water. Every animal, from birds to squirrels, enjoys this oasis during the hot, dry days.

–JEAN MITCHELL, *Plant City, Florida*

Our heavy concrete birdbath was nearly impossible to clean until I discovered a simple remedy. I set a glass pie dish inside it. It's clear, so it doesn't detract from the bath's beauty. I just wash it in the dishwasher.

–DEE FANNIN, *Santa Rosa, California*

Place a few pennies in your birdbath. They slow down algae buildup.

–PATTY LOWNEY, *Appleton, Wisconsin*

Texas summers are hot, so I devised a way to provide cool water for my birds. Every night I freeze water in empty waxed milk cartons. When I come home for lunch, I put one of the blocks of ice in the birdbath. It doesn't take long for the birds to find the cool water. Then I add another fresh block when I return home in the evening.

–ERMA SHORT, *Texarkana, Texas*

Foxgloves growing
near a birdbath

American goldfinches and pine siskins share space at a tube feeder.

Since my children outgrew their swing set, I made a feeding station out of the frame. It's now equipped with a variety of feeders hung from varying lengths of wire.

–JILL HERSCH
Ayr, North Dakota

Solve the problem of spilled seed under your bird feeder by using a "holey" pizza pan. Bore a hole the size of the feeder pole in the center of the pan. Secure it with a hose clamp directly beneath the feeder. The tiny holes allow for drainage, and the birds have a second place to feed from.

–JAYNE BELL
Greenwood, South Carolina

When purchasing plants for containers, it's often cheaper to buy inexpensive hanging baskets and divide the contents to use in the garden and in containers.

Garden centers and home improvement stores often run sales on hanging baskets, and the equivalent number of individual plants would add up to much more. It's one of my favorite money stretchers to get more bloom for my buck!

–DONNA GRIFFIN
Amarillo, Texas

Baltimore oriole

We set out orange slices for the orioles and suet for the woodpeckers. But we received an added bonus when we realized catbirds enjoy both these treats, too.

–DAVE AND BONNIE DOWNS, *Dodgeville, Wisconsin*

In summer we fill our birdbaths with water that drips from our air conditioner. Using this distilled water helps reduce algae.

–CHARLEY AND JUDY SAYRE, *Newark, Ohio*

I place large colorful marbles in my birdbaths. They seem to attract more winged activity.

–DEANE TAYLOR, *Summerfield, North Carolina*

Feeders don't have to be fancy to attract lots of birds. Groups of evening grosbeaks visit my backyard when I set out a simple pie plate filled with sunflower seeds atop a kitchen stool. What's most important is to provide the proper seed and keep it coming.

–MARCY CELLA, *L'Anse, Michigan*

Black-capped chickadee

Rose-breasted grosbeak

With a few reader tips and secrets, you can
attract more summer birds

Birds were more interested in my birdbath after I moved it near a fence in my backyard. They land on a post, survey the yard, then hop to the bath. The fence provides a great spot for them to preen after they bathe, too.

–BETTY DEAVER, *Dell, Montana*

When cobs of sweet corn are too ripe to eat, I place them on my tray feeder. The birds love feasting on the kernels.

–GARY CLARK, *Knowlton, Quebec*

Place a terra-cotta saucer on a flowerpot and you'll create a simple and effective birdbath. It's shallow enough for the birds to wade in the water and also large enough to accommodate several at once.

–SHERYL NEAL, *Carrollton, Ohio*

In summer, I often spray water on my trees and shrubs, which keeps them healthy and also attracts winged wildlife. The mist from my hose invites hummingbirds and butterflies, while the water dripping from leaves seems to satisfy thirsty birds for hours.

–GLENDA JORDAN, *Austell, Georgia*

Instead of tube feeders, I fill mesh bags with seeds for the American goldfinches. I tie them to a decorative shepherd's hook that also holds hanging plants. The bags are inexpensive and provide perfect perches for finches.

–HILDEGARD LEMKE, *Wauwatosa, Wisconsin*

If you have a chain-link fence, use it for growing some of birds' favorite treats. I plant honeysuckle, sunflowers and cosmos along mine. It's a great way to create an interesting area in your garden while feeding birds at the same time.

–LINDA LANCASTER, *Ada, Oklahoma*

I make a simple bird feeder out of a large orange cut in half, with the fruit cleaned out. I smear peanut butter on it, and add some wild birdseed mix. I put it out in a hanging basket near my other feeders, and the birds love it.

–SUSAN SIPPLE, *Latonia, Kentucky*

Catbirds are one of my favorite backyard visitors, so it was a welcome surprise when I discovered they relish the grape jelly I put out for orioles. Although they're known as shy birds, they became friendlier as they continued to feed on the jelly throughout summer. After a while, they even kept eating as I was gardening.

–PAULA SMITS, *De Pere, Wisconsin*

Just because I live in an apartment doesn't mean I can't feed birds. I just hang window feeders from my picture windows. They're usually clear plastic and hang from suction cups. Most gardening centers have a variety of these handy little feeders.

–LISA SCOTT, *Bloomington, Indiana*

Peel one side of an apple, score it a little bit and hang it from a tree branch with wire. The finches really love the summer treat. Even butterflies stop by to feed on the juice.

–LU REED, *Spencer, Iowa*

I hang gourd birdhouses in my garden to encourage birds to stay. It's an easy and inexpensive birdhouse solution.

–RITA JEMISON, *Ashland, Mississippi*

Feed birds at the same time every day. They'll get to know your routine and greet you as you fill the feeders.

–ROBERT KAUFMAN, *McClure, Illinois*

Use a tomato cage to keep crows out of your birdbath. Just cut off the legs and place it upside down in the basin.

–MARION LEWIS, *Normandy Park, Washington*

Water attracts more birds to my yard than feeders do, so I provide lots of water dishes and birdbaths all around my yard. I have attracted doves, woodpeckers, mallards, great blue herons, snowy egrets and great egrets.

–LOU KELLEY, *Tampa, Florida*

There was little activity at my birdbath until I exchanged my white basin for a terra-cotta one. Almost immediately after I made the switch, birds began stopping by to drink.

–ANGELA MARTINEZ, *Clifton, Colorado*

Northern cardinals can't resist my seed mix of peanuts, sunflower seeds, millet and corn served on a tray feeder.

–WENDY RUPRECHT, *Cold Springs, Minnesota*

composting

Smelly compost? Just add leaves or other dry materials to the pile. Then mix. The dry matter will help dry out the pile and eliminate the smell.

–MELINDA MYERS, *Milwaukee, Wisconsin*

After several years, our heavyweight plastic totes developed splits and cracks. Since they weren't good for toting anything anymore, I converted one into a compost bin. All I did was drill several small holes in the sides for ventilation and two smaller ones in the snap-on lid.

–JOHANNA MUENCH, *Magedon, New York*

Create compost quickly by reducing the size of the materials. The bigger it is, the longer it takes to decompose. Use a lawn mower or shredder to break down garden waste or leaves whenever possible. Turning the pile once a week keeps air circulating, which also speeds up decomposition.

–JOSEPH NOVARA, *Kalamazoo, Michigan*

Leaves are a must for compost bins

Apple peels

Compost bins

Eggshells

Rich soil includes compost.

I use compost to help keep my rose garden free of weeds. After weeding, I lay several layers of newspaper down over the area, wet them down and then cover them with compost. This combination keeps the weeds from sprouting.

–ELVERA DARMER, *Andover, Minnesota*

I built my compost bin from used wood pallets. They're often free for the asking at home building centers. Plus, the spaces between the pallet boards allow air to circulate through the material in the bin.

–EARL RUBY, *West Hartford, Connecticut*

I cover the top of my compost bin with an old piece of carpet. It's a nice, inexpensive cover. Also, the materials in the bin should be as moist as a wrung-out sponge. If they're too dry, sprinkle them with a fine mist from your garden hose, but be careful not to make them too wet.

–MARION KING, *Gloucester, Ontario*

I collect kitchen scraps in a plastic canister. When it's full, I take it outside, dig a hole and bury the scraps. In a few weeks, it turns to black gold. The next time I pick a different spot. This saves a lot of time and work.

–EVELYN SHANKEN, *Murrieta, California*

Place your compost bin on a pallet with ½-inch hardware cloth stapled to the top. This provides plenty of air, and it's easy to shovel the compost right off the pallet when it's ready.

–CLYDE WALLENFANG, *Greenfield, Wisconsin*

To make easy compost, rake broken-up leaves and pack them into plastic leaf bags that you've poked holes in. Water the leaves thoroughly and tie the tops of the bags. The natural freeze-thaw cycles of our Montana winters break down the leaves into beautiful compost.

–MRS. A.C. WALLACE, *Billings, Montana*

I make compost in a heavy plastic trash can with wheels and a lock-down lid. It's lightweight, mobile and retains moisture. Several holes drilled about 7 inches apart near the top of the can provide aeration.

–BEVERLY HOWELL, *Montrose, Colorado*

Every fall I put three to four wheelbarrows full of leaves into an open compost bin and add a little soil. By the next growing season, I have a wheelbarrow full of black soil.

–INGA BURKHOLDER, *Cecil Lake, British Columbia*

I built a compost bin at the end of my small garden. Then I asked my neighbor to empty his lawn mower bag into it whenever he mows. I put my own clippings in the bin, too. It's a great way to create rich compost.

–YOLI QUEVEDO, *Anacortes, Washington*

It's said that a few branches of yarrow will help a compost pile mature faster.

–CRYSTAL WHITE, *Chesterton, Indiana*

Instead of raking leaves, use your lawn mower with a bagger to pick them up. This chops them into fine pieces and makes excellent mulch for the garden.

–MARY ANN GRABER, *Bloomfield, Indiana*

I *improved poor garden soil* by covering it with all the grass clippings I could get my hands on. (Avoid clippings from lawns that have invasive grasses or that have been recently treated with weed killers.) I went to a pasture and scooped up the cow patties to throw on, too. That spring, I could grow just about anything in that soil.

–L.D. APLIN JR., *Greenville, Texas*

fall
solutions

backyard cleanup

House wrens

Leave birdhouses up all year. Clean them in late fall and spray the inside of the birdhouse with a strong stream of water.

–SUE HENSLEY, *Lenoir City, Tennessee*

I clean my birdhouses in fall, then store them inside all winter. That way, I don't risk mice nesting in them.

–ARTHUR STEFANELLI

Fairview, Pennsylvania

Since I replaced the bottom of my birdhouse with a sliding board, cleaning is easy. I simply remove the board and the house's contents fall to the ground.

–DELLA JOHNSON

Bellingham, Washington

The easiest way to clean a birdhouse is by first soaking the inside with water using a spray bottle. Then I just scrape out the old nesting material. To avoid inhaling debris, you might want to wear a mask over your nose and mouth.

–TOM KOVACH

Park Rapids, Minnesota

Black-capped chickadee

As long as your plants didn't have any problems this year, you can clean them out and add to your compost pile.

Every fall, I put my garden to bed by raking all my leaves into it. It's easy and helps the soil.

–ANN PROFFIT, *Bellbrook, Ohio*

In fall, don't pull out the dead annuals in your garden. They'll come out much more easily in spring after the roots have rotted. If you cover your beds with leaves in fall, the annuals also help hold the leaves in place.

–JODIE STEVENSON, *Export, Pennsylvania*

Putting my garden to bed for the winter is a process that actually starts in midsummer. When annuals fade, I remove them and mulch the beds for winter. By late October, I've emptied the pots on my patio and cut back the few remaining perennials. When you make cleanup a continuous process, it isn't so overwhelming.

–MARCIA BRIGGS, *Pittsburgh, Pennsylvania*

At the end of the season, I disinfect all my tools and tomato cages with a solution of 1 part bleach to 9 parts water. This also can be used during the growing season when handling diseased plants.

–SUE GRONHOLZ, *Columbus, Wisconsin*

In fall, we take all the garden extras (vegetables, stalks, vines, etc.) and drag them to the compost pile. Then we till the garden well. In spring, we just add composted horse manure and our gardens are ready to go.

–MARTHA ODELL, *Sidney Center, New York*

For a few years now, gardeners in my area have been holding perennial parties. Each spring and fall, different gardeners take turns hosting the gathering in their backyards.

It's a great time to exchange tips, advice and plants. Roughly 150 gardeners are involved. We organize the plants by light needs and by type, such as herbs, daylilies and hostas. We have thousands of plants!

A few of the ladies involved are master gardeners. They answer questions before the trading begins. Then we take turns picking plants until they're all gone.

I've filled entire flower beds with these free plants, like the mums at right. I look forward to the event every autumn. I hope others can use this idea to start their own perennial parties.

–CONNIE BAUMANN, *Lino Lakes, Minnesota*

Chrysanthemums

Radishes

Every summer, I take photos of my garden. In fall, I mount them in a lined notebook and write comments under each photo. I record what I planted that year, plants I'd like to try and tips to improve next year's garden. It's a big help to write these things down when they're fresh in my mind. Then for spring, I'm ready.

–**KAREN ANDREWS**, *Petersburg, Ontario*

Don't spend a lot of money to create a new flower bed. Cover the area with old carpet in fall. By spring, the grass will be dead, and the soil will be moist and ready to till.

–**BARB WAGNER**, *Willmar, Minnesota*

I live between two large bodies of water, where we have some wild winter storms and a lot of snow. In the fall, I bag all of my leaves and stack them around the foundation of my house for added insulation. In spring, the leaves are the perfect mulch for my organic vegetable and flower garden.

–**LAURI WALKER**, *Sauble Beach, Ontario*

In areas with mild winters, try this fall routine for a weed-free garden next spring. Pull the spent vegetation from your beds, work in compost you've been saving since spring, and mulch with a heavy covering of marsh hay or straw. In spring, just pull back the hay and you're ready to plant your garden.

–**RUTH WEAVER.** *Joshua, Texas*

It's good to leave up some plants into fall and winter because they'll make a good food source for birds.

If you don't want to dig up dahlia tubers each fall, try my method. After the first frost, I cut down the dahlia stalks, place three layers of cardboard over the bed of tubers and cover it with 3 to 4 inches of soil to hold the cardboard in place. Then I top that with 6 to 8 inches of leaves.

After all danger of frost has passed in spring, I remove the leaves, soil and cardboard. If the tips of the plants are already peeking through the soil, I cover them with leaves or soil to protect them. With this method, I seldom lose any plants in my Zone 6 area, near Dayton. (Gardeners in more northerly areas should play it safe and bring tubers inside for winter.)

–ETHEL GEPFORD, *Miamisburg, Ohio*

Before storing them for winter, I dust gladiolus corms and dahlia tuberous roots with sulfur. (For safety, always label treated bulbs.) I store the glad corms in open trays and dahlia roots in boxes of peat moss, and I've seldom had any go bad during storage.

–JOYCE COOKSEY, *Braintree, Massachusetts*

While you're doing a little bit of yard work this fall, don't just toss all your leaves. Save a few of the nice ones for some fun craft projects. For example, you can do leaf rubbings with kids, string a few together with thread for a fall garland display or make colorful prints with paint (the leaves makes great stamps).

Whenever you deadhead your plants, throw the flower heads back into the garden. You'll often get free flowers the following spring!

I get free petunias, marigolds, snapdragons, alyssum, nicotiana, cosmos, hollyhocks, poppies and more. If you don't like where the new flowers come up, just move them or weed them out.

–PEG LAIR, *Kenyon, Minnesota*

To protect perennials from harsh winters, cover beds with landscape cloth. This allows moisture and air through while still protecting the plants. Since it blocks light, remove it as soon as plants start growing in spring. Cleanup is easy. Even my tea roses do well under this covering.

–ROBERTA CARD-CLARK, *Superior, Wisconsin*

Each fall, I put several loads of manure and all our leaves and clippings into the garden. It doesn't seem to matter whether the manure is fresh or composted. We get the same good results either way.

–DAVID HALBROOK, *Kings Beach, California*

I spread and till compost and manure on my garden, then cover the surface with newspapers and straw. In spring, there are no weeds to pull, and the garden is immediately ready to plant.

–DOROTHY SIMONS, *Bremerton, Washington*

Before cold weather arrives, take cuttings from begonias, coleus and other outside plants unable to withstand the cold. Place them in pots, and keep them in a dry, warm area, like the top of the refrigerator, until they root.

–CAROL WRIGHT, *Johnston, South Carolina*

Once you start cleaning up your garden in fall, you might be surprised at all the clay pots you've acquired. Don't toss them! Clean them up, give them a paint job and they just might make the perfect Christmas gift. (Chalkboard paint is a fun and easy way to give them new life.)

To clean rusty garden tools, I rub them with a steel-wool soap pad dipped in turpentine. Then I polish with wadded aluminum foil. I love the results!

–MARY OHMS, *Carrollton, Texas*

After raking autumn leaves into bags, I pile the bags in an out-of-the-way corner. In spring, I line the aisles of the garden with old newspaper and then cover it with the leaves. The combination of newspaper and leaves holds in moisture and minimizes weeds. It also provides a nice place to walk when the rest of the garden is muddy. In fall, all this is organic mulch, and the cycle continues.

–NITA YOUNG, *Nebo, North Carolina*

Eastern wahoo in fall

The clay in our garden soil tends to become packed. Adding maple leaves in fall helps keep it loose and moist.

–MARY MAHN, *Ravenna, Illinois*

suet recipes

Downy woodpecker

Birds love my "High Energy Double-Nut Tweety Treat." Keep in mind, however, that the recipe takes about 3 hours to complete:

5 to 7 pounds raw suet	1 cup peanut butter
1 pound fatty bacon	1 cup dry dog food, crushed
2 cups raw peanuts, chopped	1 cup sunflower hearts
2 cups raisins	½ cup sugar
2 cups cornmeal	½ cup cracked corn or mixed seed
2 cups oats	

Cook suet over stove until melted and fry bacon until crisp. Add crumbled bacon and fat to melted suet. Add remaining ingredients. Mix well.

Allow mixture to cool completely and cut into squares that fit your suet feeder.

–MARGIE HARCLERODE, *Bedford, Pennsylvania*

We replaced suet with my piecrust recipe.

The birds adore it! Mix 1 cup flour, ½ cup shortening, ¼ teaspoon salt and just enough water to form a ball. There's no need to bake it—just put the treat out near your seed feeders and watch it disappear.

–LINDA BYLER, *Middlefield, Ohio*

I've shared this suet recipe with all my friends,

and it always gets rave reviews from the birds.

2 cups peanut butter

2 cups lard

½ cup each of flour, old-fashioned oats, Spanish peanuts, raisins, sunflower seeds and chopped corn

Melt peanut butter and lard. Mix all ingredients in a large cake pan and refrigerate until hardened. Cut and place in suet feeders for your feathered friends.

–ETHEL FLEMING, *Hemphill, Texas*

Red-bellied woodpecker

This suet recipe attracts a variety of birds, including sparrows, juncos, blue jays, chickadees and woodpeckers. The birds are always fighting over it.

1 cup lard

1 cup crunchy peanut butter

⅓ cup sugar

2 cups quick cooking oats

2 cups cornmeal

1 cup flour

1 cup birdseed

Melt lard and peanut butter. Add sugar to the melted mix. Combine remaining ingredients. Form blocks and freeze.

–JOSEPH PAVELCHAK, *Robbinsville, New Jersey*

Northern mockingbird

Melt 2 cups lard with 1 cup peanut butter, then add 2 cups cornmeal.

This is a very simple recipe, but it has served me well for many years. I also like that it's easy to double or triple the quantity. I've tried fancier recipes, but this one is the cheapest, and the birds seem to like it just as well.

Sometimes I throw in nuts, raisins, crushed cereal or a little oatmeal. I almost never add seed because the seed-eating birds have the other feeders, and this keeps my suet-log feeder less crowded. The woodpeckers, nuthatches and chickadees really love it!

–HELENE MANSFIELD, *Racine, Wisconsin*

I take equal parts lard and peanut butter and melt them in the microwave, then add some quick oats, cornmeal, flour and a little sugar.

I don't have exact measurements, but if the mixture is too runny I just add another sprinkling of oats.

Once I mix everything up, I put the suet in a waxed-paper-lined cake pan and let it settle. Then I cut it into six squares and freeze it. When I need it for my suet cages, I just pull it out of the freezer. Birds in my area love this mixture more than anything you can buy at the store, and it's cheap to make.

–PATRICIA DUSS, *Stanley, Wisconsin*

This tried-and-true suet recipe attracts several species of birds to my backyard.

1 cup shortening	1 ½ cups all-purpose flour
1 cup peanut butter	1 ½ cups cornmeal
¼ cup sugar	1 ½ cups quick-cooking oats

In a medium saucepan, melt shortening and peanut butter. Add remaining ingredients one at a time and blend well. Remove the mixture from heat, and let it cool overnight. Store at room temperature until you're ready to serve.

–KATHRYN STRODE, *Gilmanton, New Hampshire*

Attract woodpeckers, as well as chickadees and nuthatches, with this tropical treat.

The best part is this suet mix won't melt when it's warm outside.

1 cup lard	2 ½ cups oats
1 cup peanut butter	2 ½ cups cornmeal
⅓ cup coconut	Raisins, nuts or birdseed, optional

Melt lard and peanut butter. Stir in coconut, oats and cornmeal. Add optional ingredients. Pour the mixture into a pan and chill in refrigerator overnight. Cut into squares and wrap in plastic for easy storage and removal.

–REBECCA BEILER, *Lancaster, Pennsylvania*

I save all the grease from any meat I cook until I have a jarful, then melt it along with peanut butter.

Then I add oats, flour, raisins, seed and anything else I have on hand, like old cereal, cookie crumbs or cornmeal.

I mix everything well, then put it in square cardboard boxes and place them in the freezer. When I'm ready to use the suet, I tear off the cardboard and place it in the suet feeders.

–LARKIE RICHERT, *Indianapolis, Indiana*

I have a good recipe to make suet cakes the birds go crazy for.

Here are the ingredients:

1 cup cornmeal	1 cup birdseed
1 cup sugar	1 cup peanut butter
½ cup flour	1 cup raisins
1 cup water	

Mix everything together in a bowl. Microwave on high for 3 minutes and then stir. Pour half of the mixture into a plastic container about the size of a square suet feeder. Press it down, put wax paper on top and then add the rest of the mixture. Put a lid on the container and freeze. The birds will love it!

–DIANA CLAPPER, *Central City, Pennsylvania*

"Birdmeal" attracts woodpeckers.

Mix 1 cup each of shortening, peanut butter and flour. Then mix in 4 cups of cornmeal. When finished, it should be the consistency of putty. Press the mixture into the bark of trees and in the corners of your feeders.

–HAROLD WEPPLER, *Atlantic, Iowa*

Here is an easy recipe to attract a variety of feathered friends.

2 cups peanut butter	2 small boxes of raisins
1 cup uncooked oats	1 cup Special K
½ cup honey	(toasted corn) cereal

Mix all ingredients together in a bowl. Smear inside your suet feeder. If you'd like, you can also refrigerate the mixture for an hour or so, and shape it into balls for a tray feeder or suet cage.

–DENISE OTERI, *Weymouth, Massachusetts*

This hearty mixture attracts a large variety of birds.

1 ½ cups wild birdseed	1 cup graham cracker crumbs
1 cup bread crumbs	2 teaspoons sand (for grit)
1 cup melted suet	

Simply mix all the ingredients together and serve on a tray feeder.

–ANN STURGEON, *Kokomo, Indiana*

Here's the easiest way to make suet for the birds: Collect excess cooking grease in a can and put it in the freezer. You can even add eggshells, cornmeal and seeds to the can as it's being filled.

When it's full, use a can opener to remove the bottom. Then punch two holes in the side of the can, near the top and bottom rims. Insert a piece of wire through the holes, wrap it around the rims and hang the can horizontally from a tree or bird feeder. (Make sure the wire won't accidentally poke your feathered friends.) It won't take long for the birds to clean it out.

–JANET MAKI, *Cohasset, Minnesota*

Here's an alternative suet recipe that doesn't require animal fat. Give it a try in your suet feeder this fall.

1 ½ cups peanut butter	¼ cup oatmeal
1 cup wild birdseed	1 ½ tablespoons flour

Mix together ingredients, adding raisins or other dried fruit if you want. Then press the ingredients into small plastic containers. After an hour ro so in the freezer, they should be ready to pop out and put in a suet cage. Or store them until ready for use.

–LUKE LEE, *Swainsboro, Georgia*

The neat thing about this suet is that it appeals to a wide range of birds.

I've even observed robins trying to get at it! In fact, I have a hard time keeping up with the demand.

2 cups lard	4 cups cornmeal
1 cup birdseed	4 cups rolled oats
2 cups crunchy	1 cup raisins
peanut butter	⅔ cup sugar

Slowly heat the lard and peanut butter to soften them, then add remaining ingredients. Place scoops of the mixture in small plastic bags, flatten and refrigerate or freeze.

–LIZ LIST, *Greenville, South Carolina*

I make this treat for birds that visit our place in winter. It helps replace the energy they're burning as they try to stay warm.

2 quarts water	1 cup peanut butter
1 cup lard	Wheat germ, birdseed, sunflower
4 cups dry cereal	seeds or wheat bran, optional

Bring water and lard to a boil. Add cereal and cook for 15 minutes. Remove from heat and mix in peanut butter and optional ingredients.

Line plastic containers with plastic wrap and fill with the mixture. Place in freezer so it sets.

We'll often press the mixture into pinecones and hang them from tree branches near our picture windows.

–NANCY WAKELAND, *Entiat, Washington*

Make this "bird cake" treat and hang it from trees or bird feeders in mesh bags.

1 cup lard	2 cups whole wheat flour
1 cup crunchy peanut butter	1 cup oats
1 cup honey	2 eggs

Mix all ingredients and pour into a greased 9-inch square pan. Bake at 350° for 30 to 40 minutes or until a toothpick inserted in the center comes out clean.

–MARY HOCHSTETLER, *Milford, Indiana*

I make this fruity suet for my feathered friends. Mix melted lard with chopped oranges, raisins, seeds and peanuts. Pour into tuna or cat food cans and store in your refrigerator. The birds can't resist it, especially on cold winter days.

–TONJA KARNES, *Hopkins, Michigan*

I save my bacon fat and then add sunflower seeds, raisins, berries (in season), peanuts and oatmeal. Then I stir everything well. Instead of freezing the suet in a temporary container, I scoop it directly into the suet feeder, which I wrap in plastic. Once it freezes, I remove the plastic and keep it in the freezer until I need it.

It's always fun to see the birds hanging on to my feeder to devour this treat. Usually woodpeckers stop by, but I once had a tree full of scarlet tanagers enjoying my suet mix, too.

–JANIS HANDLEY, *Edmond, West Virginia*

Tufted titmouse

fall gardening

Bittersweet

I like to plant assorted varieties of sedum in pots. They survive winter in our area and do well even if the containers get dry in summer. It's a great, versatile plant.

–VALERIE GIESBRECHT, *Othello, Washington*

Even though summer is fading, there are plenty of flowers and plants that thrive in the autumn weather. Give these a try.

Anemone	Lobelia
Aster	Nasturtium
Balloon flower	Pansy
Bittersweet	Phlox
Black-eyed Susan	Rose
Chrysanthemum	Russian sage
Coreopsis	Sedum
Firethorn	Sunflower
Goldenrod	Virginia creeper
Joe Pye weed	

Chrysanthemum

This perennial garden has great foliage and texture, which will transition nicely, into fall.

A few years ago, my husband and son built raised beds for my perennials. I really wanted to see my plants bloom in succession and have vibrant color all season long, so I planned my garden to include plants with many different bloom times.

My perennials include lilies, beard tongue, liatris, coneflower, blanket flower, phlox, coreopsis, lavender, Shasta daisies and a few others.

After the perennials fade, my annuals steal the show. I planted petunias, zinnias, gladioli, calla lilies, poppies, nasturtium, bachelor buttons and celosia.

I love watching the flowers come up, open and shine in a succession of blooms!

–NANCY SMITH
Johnston City, Illinois

Here at our house, we use flower beds year-round. We have raised brick beds leading up to our front door, and it's a great place to show off the season's best colors.

This is an easy project anyone can do. No matter what size your flower beds are, there's something for every season. We plant mums in fall, cabbage in winter, tulips in spring and then various annuals in summer. So don't call it quits for the year just yet. There's plenty of gardening left to do!

–KENNETH WELTY
Springfield, Virginia

I carefully dig up my favorite geraniums and bring them indoors.
I put them in a sunny window and they bloom all winter!

–TINA EITEMILLER, *via Facebook*

Here are a few tips to keep your roses beautiful throughout the growing season.

• In early spring, trim back the dead canes. Then fertilize the plants with granular rose food, working it lightly into the soil.

• Each month throughout the summer, fertilize using a balanced rose food.

• Make sure roses are well watered. To get the most out of each watering and to protect them from disease, water only at the base of the plant.

• To keep roses blooming throughout the growing season, trim off spent blooms.

• In more northerly areas, prune back to allow for winter protection. Don't prune too much, though. Your main pruning should be done in spring.

• The winters in your area will determine how you should mound or cover your roses to protect them until spring. When in doubt, it doesn't hurt to add a little extra cover.

–JEANETTE DALTON, *Mountain Grove, Missouri*

If you want your petunias to last throughout summer, try my easy approach.
Cut back petunias in mid-July. This is good for two reasons: It keeps them short and bushy, and it also helps them bloom longer.

–MARY STAGER, *Silver May, Minnesota*

The secret to compact beautiful chrysanthemums
is to pinch back or trim about half of the plant's new growth. Repeat this until about the first week of July. And be sure to water and fertilize properly.

–MRS. LEROY MARTIN, *Hagerstown, Maryland*

To keep a garden in bloom for a long time, alternate your rows
with flowers that bloom at different times. One good combination is dahlias, gladioli and zinnias.

–LIZ MCCAIN, *Florence, Oregon*

To keep your hanging fuchsia basket full of blooms,
pinch off spent flowers. Do this constantly and the plant will bloom all summer.

–MARGARET LINDOW, *Suamico, Wisconsin*

Rosebush blooms don't have to be short-lived.
After a rosebush blooms and the flowers fade, I cut the flowering stems down to the next leaf with five leaflets. The plant often continues to bloom into late summer and sometimes early fall.

–JAN GRAGE, *Centerville, South Dakota*

Have you ever tried starting a new rosebush from a cutting? Give it a shot with Julie's suggestion, below.

If you live in an area with mild winters, it's easy to start new rosebushes from your existing ones. Whenever you prune them, just use the cuttings to root new plants.

You can dip the tips of the cuttings into rooting hormone first, but I've had success just planting them right in the soil. With this easy method, my garden is always filled with beautiful roses.

–JULIE SOILEAU, *Marbury, Alabama*

Here's a hint for keeping a new perennial bed vibrant all summer long: Interplant it with colorful annuals. The annuals will fill in the bare spots until your perennials get established. If your perennial garden is in its second or third year, plant the annuals in pots and add them wherever you'd like color.

–**MARIE BLAHUT**, *Yorkton, Saskatchewan*

When you trim your chrysanthemums back in summer, you may be able to enjoy even more flowers later. I plant the tops I've cut off in the soil along our garage wall. Soon I have enough new plants to share with friends and neighbors.

–**MARTHA MILLER**, *Auburn Hills, Michigan*

Sunflowers (above) and dahlias (far right) both carry over nicely into fall.

I wait to plant my sunflowers until June 1.

I plant a late tomato crop in early August along with lots of zinnias, cosmos, marigolds and pansies. They love the cooler weather.

–GINNY TANEY HARNSBERGER, *via Facebook*

In autumn, when the plants in my flower box are done blooming, I fill it with dried flowers from my garden. This way I can enjoy its beauty all year round.

–VICTORIA TESCH, *Wausau, Wisconsin*

Rejuvenate old perennials by dividing them. If the center of the plant is woody and no longer produces flowers, divide it in half. Cut out and discard the center and cut the remaining ring into smaller pieces. Plant some of these pieces in the same spot, and soon you'll see new growth. Plant extra pieces in other areas, or share them with friends.

–ANGELA GRIFFIN HATCHETT, *Altoona, Alabama*

They will grow well into fall and even survive a few cold nights.

–SHELLEY SEIDMAN, *via Facebook*

attracting fall
birds & butterflies

Tufted titmouse

We buy unsalted peanuts and tuck them underneath the bark of our trees. Blue jays, nuthatches, chickadees, tufted titmice, flickers, woodpeckers and other birds hunt for the peanuts throughout our yard.

-MIKE FALLON, *Straughn, Indiana*

The birds, especially blue jays, love unsalted peanuts. I buy in bulk to save money. They flock to my feeders!

–LORRAINE FAYE ZAJAC
Mohnton, Pennsylvania

Chisel out the centers of tree stumps and fill them with nuts and seeds for ground-feeding birds and critters this fall.

–ANNETTE MACDONALD
Hampton, Ontario

A coconut is an extra-special treat for the birds. Simply split it in half, drill three evenly spaced holes around the rim and hang it. We fill ours with seed and bacon grease, too.

–ELAINE WADE
Jackson, Michigan

Hollow out your pumpkins and fill them with cracked corn and birdseed to give ground-feeding birds a special autumn treat.

–GLORIA MEREDITH
Harrington, Delaware

Blue jays

Common sulfur butterfly on
butterfly weed

When you visit a garden center and see butterflies

and bees flitting around, pay attention to the types of plants they're visiting. Buy those for your yard.

–JANE EMRICH UMSTEAD, *via Facebook*

A little bit of this and a little bit of that is the trick to wooing birds

I love nooks and crannies. My favorite thing is to add a birdbath, bird feeder, birdhouse, and if the spot is shady, a big pot of impatiens. If it's a sunny area, I'll substitute salvia. The birds, squirrels, hummingbirds and butterflies add a lot of life to those lifeless areas.

–**LINDA CARTER,** *Pearl River, Louisiana*

Monarch butterflies east of the Rocky Mountains migrate to Mexico in fall. To provide help sustain them as they fly south, I plant goldenrod and lantana, both excellent sources of nectar.

–**MARLENE CONDON,** *Crozet, Virginia*

Pecans are a favorite of the birds in my yard. Since they're expensive, I wait until mine have lost their fresh taste. Then I put a handful in a mesh bag and hang it from a tree limb. It doesn't take long for the birds to find this treat.

–**MARY WESTMORELAND,** *Snyder, Texas*

I live in western Minnesota, where pileated woodpeckers are common in fall and winter. Normally very shy, solitary birds, they especially like suet feeders.

The suet cakes that work best for us are the ones with plenty of seed and peanuts. We don't offer just one, though. We place several suet feeders out within 10 feet of one another, which seems to attract the most woodpeckers.

These woodpeckers feed for three to five minutes before flying off, which allows me some time for photos. I hope our tips help others attract this great bird.

–**ROGER LEE,** *Fergus Falls, Minnesota*

When using egg whites, don't throw out the yolks. Scramble them, cool and put them in your feeder. It gives the birds extra calcium.

–**NANCY SPEAR,** *Gilford, New Hampshire*

Birds really enjoy hickory nuts. All you have to do is find a way to break their rock-hard shells. I hold them with pliers, hit them with a hammer (wear safety goggles) and place the broken pieces—shells and all—in my feeders. The birds pick out the meats.

–**KENNETH SEARFOSS,** *Reading, Pennsylvania*

Serve dried corncobs to wildlife by driving a large nail halfway into the top of a post. Cut the head off with a bolt cutter and spear the ear onto the spike. Squirrels love this, too!

–**CHRISS STUTZMAN,** *Navarre, Ohio*

Milbert's tortoiseshell on summersweet

I place a handful of peanuts on my deck whenever I see blue jays in the backyard. As a result, they now associate me with food and often come to the patio door looking for me.

–**CONNIE COLOUTES,** *Poland, Ohio*

Spread this mixture onto an empty sunflower head.

1 cup water
Yellow cornmeal
½ cup oats
½ cup peanut butter
Wild birdseed

Boil water and mix in just enough cornmeal to cook into a soft mixture. Remove from heat and add oats, peanut butter and birdseed. Make sure the mixture doesn't get too thick. Press into sunflower heads and hang from a tree or bird feeder.

–**GLORIA MEREDITH,** *Harrington, Delaware*

We provide plenty of cover for birds in our backyard with trees and shrubs. Our favorites are Norway spruce and yew. The birds flee to the dense branches whenever they sense there is danger.

–**CONNIE GARLAND,** *Greenwood, Indiana*

Offer pea-sized pieces of cat food, stale nuts and dried fruits on a flat surface. Birds, especially blue jays, flock to this treat.

–**TINA JACOBS,** *Wantage, New Jersey*

Northern cardinal

Pileated woodpecker

Black-capped chickadee

Our woodpecker peanut feeders always attract lots of birds, including nuthatches. It seems many birds enjoy picking at the nuts through the wire mesh.

–STACY DORSETT, *Macomb, Illinois*

White-breasted nuthatch

Nothing brings in the birds like our crab apple trees.

Northern mockingbirds, American robins, cedar waxwings and others eat the fruits.

–CHARLOTTE CLARK, *Glenpool, Oklahoma*

Cedar waxwing on serviceberry

Dark-eyed junco

Pine grosbeak

To provide winter sustenance for birds, I make sure to keep plenty of rosebushes and spirea shrubs in my garden. A variety of feathered friends stop to dine on the rose hips and spirea seeds after most of their other food sources have disappeared.

–INGA BURKHOLDER, *Cecil Lake, British Columbia*

Chickadees feed on the seeds from the huge sunflowers I plant throughout my backyard. I leave the stalks standing all winter so the little birds can continue stopping by for snacks.

–LINDA BORASIO-WOLFE, *Parma, Ohio*

My husband attaches cedar branches to our bird feeder posts. These serve as perches where birds can wait their turn to feed and also provide protection from predators. Plus, they give a lovely natural appearance to the feeding station.

–BARB PEACHEY, *Denver, Pennsylvania*

Rather than removing a dead tree, cut off any dangerous branches and leave the substantial trunk for woodpeckers to use as a nesting and feeding site. These birds are rapidly losing their natural habitat.

–LOUAINE LEISCHING, *Hendersonville, North Carolina*

Woodpeckers seem to prefer wooden feeders because they're much easier for them to grip.

–GLEN JONES, *Decatur, Georgia*

I place fruit slices in my suet basket. The woodpeckers enjoy the special snack, and the basket works perfectly.

–RICHELE HERIGAN, *Harrisburg, Pennsylvania*

My chain-link fence helps me attract birds. Every morning, I slice a few apples and an orange. Then I spear the fruit onto the top of the fence. Blue jays, northern cardinals, northern mockingbirds and woodpeckers arrive to feast.

–DAVID DUNN, *Baton Rouge, Louisiana*

I often see American goldfinches flocking around my cosmos, especially in autumn as the plants go to seed. I've counted at least a dozen finches bouncing from one stem to another in search of seeds.

–CHERIE BOULTON, *Hayward, California*

I don't change my feeding patterns much from spring to summer and fall. I just make sure to have plenty of seed, suet and water for the birds, and it keeps them coming.

—DIANE MARSHALL SCARPONI, *via Facebook*

I attract a wide variety of birds by adding orange, almond and vanilla extracts to the seed mix. After combining seeds and nuts in a giant bowl, I pour in the extracts—about 3 to 4 tablespoons of imitation vanilla extract and 1 tablespoon each of almond and orange extract for every 10 pounds of seed mix. Toss together, and the birds will line up for this special treat.

—DEBBY BAKER, *East Rochester, New York*

When cobs of sweet corn are too ripe to eat, I place them on my tray feeder. The birds love feasting on the kernels.

—GARY CLARK, *Knowlton, Quebec*

We left two dead spruce trees in our yard because they provide a buffet of bugs for downy, hairy and pileated woodpeckers.

—GINA PHILLIPS, *Wolfville, Nova Scotia*

I wait until spring before I pull the old flower plants. Birds gather in the dried-up plants to eat seeds. My coneflowers were loaded with goldfinches this year, and chickadees pecked at the rose hips.

—LU SCHMIDT, *via Facebook*

I feed only black-oil sunflower seeds to the birds. This attracts the biggest variety of visitor. I also plant pansies and impatiens, which attract both butterflies and hummingbirds.

—DEBRA CAUDILL FOSTER, *via Facebook*

House finches and goldfinches love the seedpods left on our crepe myrtles.

—JANE STEPP, *via Facebook*

One day I noticed one of my sunflower heads completely picked clean and realized it was a perfect spot to sprinkle thistle. Five minutes after I filled the sunflower head with seeds, the goldfinches had found it and were enjoying their food.

—NOREEN HELMERS, *Walton, Kentucky*

To keep sunflower heads for the birds in the fall and winter, cover the heads with stockings when they set seed. This saves the bulk of the seeds for the hungry birds that stay through fall and winter. Once the cold weather hits, simply remove the stockings and let the birds feast.

—WILBUR JENSEN, *Onalaska, Wisconsin*

To attract woodpeckers, I "planted" a dead tree in my yard and turned it into a bird buffet.

I drilled 1-inch holes along the trunk and filled them with suet and peanut butter. Then I attached a few nails and hung orange and apples halves on them. If you choose a tree about the same diameter as a telephone pole, the woodpeckers may even nest in it.

—TONJA KARNES, *Hopkins, Michigan*

The Granny Smith apple tree in our yard is a favorite place for the birds, so we leave some of the fruit on the tree for them. This is really great when all the leaves fall in autumn. Then we have a perfect view of our feathered friends snacking on the tart apples.

—MARJORIE HENRY, *Portland, Oregon*

I entice the chickadees, cardinals and blue jays to my yard by putting out sunflower seeds and pecan pieces.

—KATHRYN BALUKIEWICZ RUSSELL, *via Facebook*

I use a standard wire cooling rack for baking to attract birds. Simply hang the rack from a feeder and insert peanuts between the wires. The blue jays love it.

–R. PUTERBAUGH, *Dayton, Ohio*

Blue jay

nter

solutions

Blue jay

attracting winter birds

To provide birds with water in winter, I use a heated pet dish. It comes equipped with a thermostat and insulation. Since the bowl is quite deep, I place a rock in the water to provide a surface for the birds to stand on.

–ROLAND JORDAHL, *Pelican Rapids, Minnesota*

Eastern bluebirds

Northern cardinal

After I cut down a tree on my property, I realized too late that it had been a favorite spot for a pileated woodpecker. So I decided to "plant" the trunk in a different area of my yard. Now woodpeckers continue to hammer on the dead tree.

–HAROLD KOTH
Tomahawk, Wisconsin

We tried several times to attract songbirds into our backyard, but we kept luring unwelcome "bully" birds instead. Finally, I developed the perfect system.

I made a small enclosure out of stucco wire and surrounded it with Christmas trees that were unsold during the holiday season. This homemade forest attracts about 15 species of birds, including juncos, towhees, house finches, song sparrows and chickadees. It also provides protection from hawks and cats.

The trees last almost until June, and then I replace them with discarded branches from a neighbor's pruning.

–SALLY ANDERSON
Port Alberni, British Columbia

Submersible birdbath heaters are a quick and easy way to provide water to birds when the weather is below freezing. The best part is you can use your existing birdbath. I always place a couple of large stones in the birdbath, giving them a place to land.

–HELEN BARNARD, *Kalispell, Montana*

Blue jay

Get more traffic with a birdbath

Try these reader-tested tips.

To provide water for birds in winter, I fill a metal bucket with hot ash from my fireplace. Then I'll take the ash outside and set a metal dish on top of the bucket and fill it with water. The ashes keep the water from freezing for quite a while.

–ERMA EVANS, *Garfield, Alabama*

I set a dish filled with water on a barrel located just below a window. Because the water freezes quickly, I just open the window, remove the ice that accumulates in the dish and refill it. It's very convenient, and the birds appreciate my extra effort.

–MARGARET RETZ, *Boyceville, Wisconsin*

In northern climates, providing fresh water for birds can be difficult when temperatures drop below freezing. We have solved this problem using a heating cable normally used to prevent water pipes from freezing. The cable is wrapped around a birdbath, placed in an insulated box and plugged into an electrical outlet.

Because there is a sensor attached to the cable, it only uses electricity when water temperatures drop below freezing, as opposed to commercial water heating units, which require continuous use of electricity. This water heater not only provides fresh water to the birds but is environmentally friendly, too.

–EMERY AND ELEANOR DOWNING, *Montague, Prince Edward Island*

Because the water in my birdbath always freezes in the winter, I've started using a heated dog water dish instead. I place it on top of my cement birdbath and put a clay pot inside for the birds to stand on while they drink. Now the birds can enjoy a drink even during the coldest winter days, and it was a cost-effective solution.

–DAGMAR BOWEN, *Dover, Pennsylvania*

Finding a way to keep water warm in the winter can be difficult, especially if you don't want to spend money on an expensive heated birdbath. I've come up with a great, inexpensive way to keep water from freezing, even on the coldest winter days. You only need three things.

First, take a 2 ½-pound coffee can and drill three evenly spaced holes about an inch from the top. Then take a small candle and place it in an empty tuna or cat food can. Light the candle and place it in the bottom of the coffee can.

Next, fill a pie plate with water and place it on top of the coffee can. The heat from the candle will keep the water warm for several hours, and the birds in your backyard can have fresh water throughout the winter.

–LOUIS BUSCHER JR., *Sandwich, Massachusetts*

We have a simple combination that keeps woodpeckers visiting our yard all winter long. First of all, we keep the suet feeders filled year-round. This attracts all kinds of woodpeckers, including red-bellied, pileated and northern flickers.

Secondly, we offer water. The heated birdbath brings in lots of traffic. It seems simple, and it is! With a little food and water, the woodpeckers are never far away.

–STEVE AND GRETCHEN LANGLIE, *Chisago City, Minnesota*

Use an old slow cooker as a winter birdbath. At a low setting, water will not freeze. Since it's still a bit deep, I set a piece of lattice across the top of mine, so birds can sit on it while they drink.

–AUDREY SAMPLAWSKI, *Chetek, Wisconsin*

I made a wooden box and enclosed a floodlight. Then I cut an 8-inch centered circle in the box top, just large enough to fit an 8-inch clay dish. I fill the dish with water every morning, and the light is enough to keep the water from freezing all day long.

–CLIFFORD SMITH, *Marysville, Michigan*

Don't have shelter for birds? Here are several reader secrets for providing safe havens in winter.

I use an old skylight to create a safe feeding station. Sturdy four-by-fours support it at the corners.

–AUDREY CHURCHILL, *Springfield, Oregon*

In winter, we attach branches cut from cedar trees to our feeders to offer added protection.

–SUE BOGART, *Topeka, Kansas*

I turn my hanging flower baskets into "birdie hotels" for roosting on cold winter nights.

–KAREN COFER, *Gainesville, Georgia*

I gather cornstalks from my garden and weave them through loose wire fencing stuck into the ground around my feeders. They block wind and predators.

–GLENN ORCHARD, *Amherstburg, Ontario*

Provide extra safety at your feeders during winter by attaching wide Plexiglas to the roofs of your bird feeders.

–RICHARD SNYDER, *Emmaus, Pennsylvania*

I offer shelter for birds wintering in my backyard by leaving roosting boxes and nesting ledges up year-round.

–GLORIA MEREDITH, *Harrington, Delaware*

Cedar waxwing

Black-capped chickadee

White-winged crossbill

In winter, nandina, holly and juniper often hold on to their fruit.

A lot of birds are attracted to the fruit as the temperature drops.

–EMILY GREY, *Onancock, Virginia*

feeding winter birds

Dark-eyed junco

*Dark-eyed juncos don't visit unless
I throw some seed on the ground.* So
I scatter cracked corn below my feeders. This also
attracts other ground feeders, like mourning doves,
northern cardinals and various sparrows.

–WILLIAM YODER, *Guthrie, Kentucky*

Cardinals

I save grease from bacon and other meats
in a refrigerated container. When winter gets especially
frigid, I'll place the hardened fat at my feeders for my feathered friends.

–JILL HERSCH, *Ayr, North Dakota*

Evening grosbeaks often show up at your feeder in winter when other birds won't. Keep your seed level up. You never know when an unexpected visitor might arrive.

During the winter it's too difficult for us to fill our bird feeders. So we convert our window boxes into feeders. We line them with pine boughs and place pinecones, birdseed and slices of apples and oranges on top to help supplement the birds' diets.

–LINDA MARTIN
Boise, Idaho

For a sweet winter bird treat, I tightly pack a snowball and drizzle maple syrup or honey on it. I leave a few on my tray feeders, and the birds love them.

–ANNE FAUVEL
Rapid City, South Dakota

A long-handled windshield scraper makes a handy tool for cleaning bird feeders in winter. It works especially well if you have lots of tray feeders.

–LYNNE MCLERNON
Lake Geneva, Wisconsin

Make sure winter feeders are filled at dawn and dusk. That's when the birds are stocking up on food. They spend most of their energy during the night, so many need to refuel first thing in the morning. They'll also load up in the evening so that they have enough fuel to carry them through the cold night.

–KEITH RUNYON
Havana, Illinois

Birds love fruit in winter. I'll offer apples, grapes, cherries, oranges, bananas and grapefruits—whatever's on sale at the grocery store. Cut round fruits, like apples and oranges, into ½-inch disks. This makes it easier for birds to eat because they won't rock or slide around on the feeding tray.

–**RON ADLER**, *St. Peters, Missouri*

During winter, I use my picnic table as a three-tiered feeding station. I toss seed on the ground beneath the table so the birds have a sheltered place to feed. The benches and tabletop serve as tray feeders.

–**JUDITH FROEHLICH**, *Berkeley Heights, New Jersey*

We make grapevine wreaths decorated with suet balls, doughnuts, popcorn, cranberry garland and dried fruits. They're a hit with the birds and squirrels. We even gave one to my parents for Christmas. They loved all the new activity it drew to their backyard.

–**JAY AND PAULA JOHNSON**, *Duluth, Minnesota*

Pine siskins

It's cold and bitter outside, so take care of your
feathered friends.

Collect the fruits of mountain ash trees in autumn. Keep them in the refrigerator until winter, then take some outside and hold them in your open hands. Usually, I don't have to wait long for the Bohemian waxwings to eat from my hands. It's a lot of fun.

–ROBERT MORIN, *Lac-Saint-Charles, Quebec*

A snowman can make an excellent winter bird feeder. Just replace the traditional stick arms with coneflower stalks and sprinkle birdseed on the snowman's hat and at its feet. I made the face with carrots and nuts.

–LORI QUALLS, *Midland, Michigan*

After the holidays, we haul our Christmas tree outside and decorate it with goodies, like dried fruit and pinecones coated with peanut butter. We remove the top half of the tree and fasten a bird feeder to the trunk. This provides shelter and a feeding station for the birds.

–LORA RASOR, *Bradford, Ohio*

On frosty winter days, the nectar in our hummingbird feeders tends to freeze. To keep it warm, I put a Christmas stocking on top. The hummingbirds stay well fed during the holidays.

–MARY LOU DAHL, *Bremerton, Washington*

Striped and black-oil sunflower seeds are high-energy food that's perfect for feeding birds in winter.

–GLORIA MEREDITH, *Harrington, Delaware*

Use sunflower heads and evergreen trimmings to make all-natural wreaths for the birds. I use the dried sunflowers in the center and arrange the branches around it. Then I decorate it with edible garland and other treats.

–JUSTINE MORRIS, *Ravenna, Ohio*

Here are a few kitchen items you can use to attract birds. Slice apples and bananas for cardinals and catbirds. Offer cooked pasta and rice for jays, titmice and woodpeckers. Use peanut butter to attract chickadees and woodpeckers. And finally, put out some raisins for a few surprise visitors.

–ELLIE MARTIN CLIFFE, *Waukesha, Wisconsin*

Use Christmas cookie cutters to make birdseed ornaments. Just cut shapes from leftover bread and brush them with egg white. Then press them in birdseed and bake at 350 degrees for 10 minutes. Thread yarn about one-quarter inch from the top of the ornaments and hang on trees.

–MEGAN WILLIAMS, *Belleville, New York*

I've found a great new use for hanging planters leftover from the summer. I turn them into bird feeders.

To make these, I put a potted plant saucer on top of the planter and fill with seed. This planter hangs right outside my bedroom window so I can see the birds every morning when I wake up.

–CAROLE MAYHEW, *Spring Green, Wisconsin*

Alaska winters mean short daylight hours, making it hard to find time to fill the feeders. So I've come up with a feeder that holds 17 pounds of seed and can go several days before a refill. I use a 5-gallon water jug, like those found in most offices, and attach a flowerpot saucer to the top and bottom. Hung from a tree outside or set on the ground, this feeder attracts red-breasted nuthatches, black-capped chickadees, pine grosbeaks, sparrows and an occasional magpie.

–WILLIAM H. DRAUGHN, *Chugiak, Alaska*

I had some leftover logs from building my log cabin, so I decided to use one to feed birds. We drilled 1-inch holes all over the log and filled them with a mixture of peanut butter and oatmeal. Within a few minutes, we had all kinds of birds paying a visit to our log. Our favorites are the woodpeckers; we've had the northern flicker, red-bellied, downy, hairy and pileated.

–JAMES GATES, *Lemoyne, Pennsylvania*

After the growing season ends, I empty my window boxes into a compost bin and turn them on their sides to use as feeding shelters. They protect the seed from wind and snow. The birds also appear comfortable dining in their protection.

–MARGARET CAPSTICK, *Sarnia, Ontario*

Don't forget to shovel a walkway to your feeders when clearing snow from your sidewalk or driveway. This makes it a lot easier to fill empty feeders when the drifts begins to pile up.

–ADRIENNE WIECZOREK, *Orland Park, Illinois*

Northern cardinal

I made a bird feeder by removing both ends of a coffee can and covering them partly with sheet metal. The seeds are protected from the harshest weather.

–DAN BARBER, *Export, Pennsylvania*

Pileated woodpeckers are common visitors in our backyard. My secret is to offer them some good old-fashioned suet—with a few extras. My special treat includes baked goods, bread crumbs, sunflower seeds and a dab of peanut butter. The squirrels leave it alone, and all my resident birds go wild for it.

–NICK RADLINSKI, *Cedar Springs, Michigan*

Bundling up in winter to fill my feeders isn't one of my favorite chores. So I hang the feeders on shepherd's hooks within a foot of my windows. I can reach out and fill the feeders, all without leaving the warmth of my home.

–JODIE STEVENSON, *Export, Pennsylvania*

In our area, many people participate in the Scandinavian Christmas tradition of hanging bundles of oats or wheat from trees for the birds. Each year we gather and decorate bundles of wheat to give to our friends for Christmas presents. It's a great way to feed the birds, draw them close to your home and carry on this tradition.

–DARWIN ANTHONY, *Trimont, Minnesota*

Don't prune vegetation until spring. This provides more shelter and food for birds.

–ANNETTE MACDONALD, *Hampton, Ontario*

During winter, I crumble the toast crusts that my four teenagers discard and toss them onto our shed roof where my dog and the squirrels can't reach them, but birds can.

–THERESE BOILEAU, *Hull, Quebec*

A simple way to feed the birds is to hollow out a loaf of unsliced bread and fill it with a mixture of peanut butter, shortening and cornmeal. The birds love it!

–JOAN CAROL BAKER, *Hope, Maine*

American robin

Lids make great bird feeding accessories. First I take the lid from an empty peanut butter jar and use a hot ice pick to put a hole through the side. Then I loop a piece of wire through it.

I fill the lid about two-thirds full of peanut butter and then drop it into a big bag of birdseed. After it is covered with seed, I take it out to my deck and hang it from a nail.

I love the results! I have several different colors of lids out there. This is a really quick, inexpensive and colorful way to make your own feeder for your favorite woodpecker friends.

–LORRENE PIERSON, *Marionville, Missouri*

Woodpeckers are some of my favorite birds at our feeders. We mostly have downy woodpeckers, but as it gets colder, we start seeing sapsuckers and red-bellied visitors.

One of our woodpeckers' favorite treats are what we call corn sticks. I know people use pinecones stuffed with peanut butter to attract birds, so I developed a little twist.

I put out squirrel corn for the bushy-tailed critters, and when they're finished with the ears, I put them to further use. I smear the ears with peanut butter, roll them in cornmeal and then attach them to a wooden pole or tree. Woodpeckers love it! They peck away at the sticks all day. Every once in a while, a tufted titmouse or a wren sneaks in for a treat, too.

–BARBARA BERRY, *Iva, South Carolina*

To protect our birds and feeders, we strap an umbrella to the pole of our shepherd's hook.

–SHIRLEY SAVIDGE, *Indianapolis, Indiana*

You can feed your feathered friends and be festive, too. First I buy an evergreen wreath, and then I place a birdseed wreath in the middle. I add a few touches like holly berries, and then sit back and wait for the birds to arrive.

They must like the edible decoration—I always have lots of visitors. It's a quick feeder solution that always puts me in the holiday spirit.

–DARLENE LAUSE, *Fort Jennings, Ohio*

Steller's jay

We don't let our Christmas tree go to waste after the holidays. If you set it outside, it can make a great treat for the birds! We made this into a family activity by filling the branches with peanut butter and birdseed. It was a fun activity and the birds really ate it up!

–CORINNE ROBERTS, *Topsfield, Massachusetts*

Common redpoll

American tree sparrow

Years ago my husband attached a shelf just outside our window for the birds and me. I fill it with sunflower seed and cracked corn. To fill it, all I have to do is open the window. Our grandchildren like this close-up view of the birds.

–MAXINE WITTE, *Rhineland, Missouri*

Birds have to look harder to find food during winter, but not in my yard. I keep my feeder filled and provide extra plates of fruit for them. I simply set a heavy log on the ground beneath my feeder. To the log, I nail a couple of aluminum pie plates and load them up with apples, oranges, raisins and cranberries.

–MARY FARLOW, *Milton, Wisconsin*

I've fed birds suet blocks for many years. But a less expensive way to satisfy their suet appetite is to simply spread lard on the bark of trees. They love it, and it's a fun way to watch them.

–BRUCE SCHAFFNER, *Cochrane, Wisconsin*

Eastern bluebirds

It's best to try hand-feeding black-capped chickadees in winter when natural sources of food are not as abundant. The ideal spot is a quiet backyard or empty hiking trail. I like to look for a tree or spot where there already is a chickadee or two. Then I simply pour some sunflower seeds into my hand and hold it out so the birds can see. The most important part of success is this—stand very still!

    –A. ANTONOW, *St. John's, Newfoundland*

I was watching my feathered friends try to hang on to a standard suet feeder when I decided they would have an easier time eating if they had a perch. That's when I hit on an idea.

    I pushed two 8-inch dowel rods through the bottom corner of the suet feeders, and then I wired two more rods across those to create a perch on each of the four sides.

    I know woodpeckers don't need the perches to eat, but it sure has increased the traffic at my suet feeders. Juncos, Carolina wrens and even downy woodpeckers seem to appreciate my "sit-down" lunch counter.

    –ALVON ABBOTT, *Warsaw, Indiana*

A great winter bird feeder can be built with a plastic colander. Simply string a few lengths of wire through its top holes or handles and hang it from a branch or shepherd's hook. Fill with seed and let the birds enjoy. The tiny holes allow melted snow to drain and help the seeds dry quickly.

    –KATHY SCARBRO, *Mount Hope, West Virginia*

Downy woodpecker

My feeding station attracts as many as 100 birds in a single day. My method is simple. I offer my feathered friends plenty of choices from my menu, including sunflower seeds, suet cakes, peanuts, raisins, fruits and nuts.

In the winter months, I buy raw beef suet, which is a favorite of the red-bellied woodpecker. Nearly all of the birds in my backyard can find something they like.

–ALEXIS ADAMS, *East Hartford, Connecticut*

Northern flicker

DIY projects

Create a wreath or seed ornaments—or designate an entire tree for your feathered friends during the holidays.

Instead of throwing away the scarves I don't wear any longer, I wrap them around my pots and containers for added flair. I do the same for my indoor plants that don't have flowers. One other idea is to use them to dress up a snowman.

–ANNA VICTORIA REICH
Stafford, Virginia

To clean vases or flower containers that have many small nooks, I use an effervescent denture cleaning tablet. I just let it sit and bubble in water for a few hours, and soon the vase is sparkling. Then I rinse it thoroughly, and it's ready to use again.

–FRAN PARR, *Eldon, Missouri*

The winters here are long, so I began looking for a new art project to spend time waiting for spring. I have worked with clay for many years, so I made my own flowerpots. I used recycled materials and leftover paint to design them. They brighten up the shady spots in my yard and only look expensive.

–BEVERLY CHRISTENSEN, *Greene, Iowa*

I recently became interested in creating mosaics using cut glass. Being a bird enthusiast, one of my first projects was a new bird feeder for spring. I snipped and glued the glass, included a few opaque beads for a raised texture, and finally grouted and painted it.

–IRENE BAKER, *Vail, Arizona*

For a pretty display, place dried flowers in a bottle, pour in oil, and seal.

–ELIZABETH STRUTOWSKI, *Mesa, Arizona*

An oversized cup and saucer make a perfect container for houseplants.

Fall maple leaves

To extend your garden's season, preserve flowers and leaves using a flower press or any large heavy book.

Ferns press well, as do coreopsis, violets, Queen Anne's lace, delphinium, phlox, salvia, buttercups and pansies.

It's easy to do. Just pick the flowers when they're in full bloom and cut the stems below the blossoms. Then lay flowers upside down on blotting paper or white typing paper. Cover with another sheet of paper and tighten the press or close the book. (Use several sheets of paper when using a book to avoid damaging its pages.) Flowers should be dry in two to three weeks.

Dried flowers and leaves can be used to decorate pillar candles, or they can be glued onto heavy paper and framed. Other popular crafts include bookmarks, stationery and greeting cards. To make these yourself, simply glue flowers onto paper and cover with clear Con-Tact paper. They're easy to do, inexpensive and make great gifts.

–JUDY HOOLSEMA, *Portage, Michigan*

I made inexpensive steppingstones by lining a springform cake pan with plastic wrap, then filling it with cement. Before it dried, I had my children make a handprint or footprint in each one. Then we decorated them with rocks, marbles and anything else we could find. We plan to add new steppingstones each year.

–MARY SCHMIDT, *Hawarden, Iowa*

I made a festive feeder using a green 2-liter bottle and a red plastic funnel. Use the funnel as the top of the feeder and then decorate it with a colorful bow, artificial greenery and brass bells. It looks so pretty against the glistening white snow.

–JOANNE SAUTER, *Ironwood, Michigan*

If you're like me, you probably have lots of plants in your garden that came from friends. The only problem with that is that it can be difficult to remember the names of all those new plants.

I have lots of photos of my garden, so whenever I receive a new nursery or seed catalog, I page through it, looking for pictures of any mystery plants. When I match them up, I cut out the information and tape it to the back of my photos for future reference.

–DAWN NEIBARGER, *Mio, Michigan*

Make yourself a garden bench with a seat that lifts to reveal a deep storage area for potting soil, leaf bags and garden tools. Besides beautifying your yard and providing a spot for a rest break, a bench like this will save you lots of trip to the toolshed or garage.

–DAWN HANN, *Red Hill, Pennsylvania*

My mother put her stacks of old magazines to good use by decorating the back and seat of an old bench with the photos. She used a decoupage technique with the photos, and then painted the rest of the bench blue.

–HOLLY MONROE, *Columbia, Missouri*

To stretch our birdseed budget, we decided to save aluminum cans, crush them and sell them at the recycling center. Whatever cash we get from the cans we now set aside for the birdseed. It's a great way to recycle while treating the birds.

–JUDIE MYERS, *Springfield, Ohio*

I made my own centerpiece for our holiday dinner with a homegrown gourd. It was the perfect shape to make a little turkey, and my family loved it.

–JILL BOSTWICK, *Chehalis, Washington*

Get ready for nesting season with these clever seed eggs. Start making these bird treats indoors to get ready for the spring season!

⅓ cup gelatin

1 ½ cups water

8 cups birdseed

Mix gelatin and water over low heat until the gelatin is melted and clear. Remove from heat and stir in birdseed. Stir until there is no dry seed. Form mixture into egg shapes. Refrigerate for two to four hours and dry on baking rack for three days.

–ANGIE DIXON, *Blaine, Washington*

Recycle your Christmas tree—and protect bulbs and perennials at the same time. Cut off branches and lay them in the garden, with the branches overlapping each other about 6 inches. If the soil is soft, push branches in so they won't blow away. If the ground is frozen, you may need to cover the branches with fine mesh or netting to hold them in place.

–ROSE MARIE CASALE, *Hasbrouck Heights, New Jersey*

BASIL

BASIL

RED BASIL

I recycle large coffee cans and use them as flowerpots. I spray-paint them and sometimes add painted scenes or decals. They're especially nice to use when giving a plant as a gift.

–ANN WARD, *Naples, Florida*

indoor gardening

African violet

Even though it might be cold outside, you can still continue gardening indoors during the winter months. In fact, it's a great time to start your garden early.

In late December and early January, I turn half of my kitchen and dining area into a hothouse, complete with shelving and lights.

I start by planting seeds in egg cartons. Then I cover them with plastic and put them on my shelves. As the plants get taller, I put old toilet paper rolls around the growing plants for support.

After the last frost date passes in spring, I plant my veggies outside. Then I get to enjoy fresh vegetables a lot earlier.

Winter can be a great time to garden— you just have to get a little creative. It's fun to do and will keep you gardening year-round.

–HOWARD BOHNE
North Charleston, South Carolina

Mums

My grandmother taught me to save money on annuals by taking "slips" of plants in the fall. I make cuttings from healthy plants, root them in water or a well-drained potting mix, then grow in a sunny window all winter. By spring, they're ready to set out.

–SHARON BRADSHAW, *Richmond, Missouri*

Trumpet vine

Potted summer flowers in old steel frying pan base

Wintering geraniums is fairly easy with my method. Before frost hits, pull them up and place in brown grocery bags. Store under the basement stairs with the bags open. At potting time, trim to 4 to 6 inches, place in pots and put back under the stairs. When plants begin to grow, they're ready to set outside, but they may need to be protected from the cold.

–JOSEPHINE SLEMMONS, *Jackson, Michigan*

Use coffee grounds and leftover coffee on your houseplants and watch them thrive. I've been doing this for a long time, and it really works.

–DELORES KOLAND, *Pelican Rapds, Minnesota*

Our houseplants survived our month-long vacation, even though we didn't have anyone to water them.

I watered the plants thoroughly, then put each one inside its own clear plastic trash bag. I left plenty of air in the bags and tied ribbons around the tops to secure them. I set the plants out of the sun, turned the thermostat down to 55° and took off.

When we returned four weeks later, the flowering plants were blooming. We had 15 plants, and all of them looked beautiful except for one vine that didn't do well.

–MAE BIEMERET, *Watersmeet, Michigan*

When changing the water in your aquarium, don't throw it out! Use it on your houseplants or outdoor plants. It gives them a boost and is much cheaper than commercial fertilizer.

–EMMA FRASER, *Ludlow, Maine*

When plant leaves get dusty, clean them with a rag dipped in milk.

It leaves them shiny and is much cheaper than commercial sprays.

–DIANE LEE, *Richland Center, Wisconsin*

Use room-temperature or warm water when watering houseplants.

This prevents them from going into shock and keeps them healthy.

–DARLENE WYNESS

Williams Lake, British Columbia

When I plant my amaryllis in the garden come summer, I leave them in pots.

In fall, I just pull the pots out and bring them in the basement, where they lie on their sides for six to eight weeks. Once the bulbs begin to sprout, I plant them in fresh soil, bring them upstairs and place in a bright window. Then I give them a good drink to help start their growing season.

–VIVIAN MCCORKLE, *Smithville, Missouri*

To save geraniums through winter, gently dig out the plants before a killing frost.

Shake off the soil and place them in brown paper bags. After a couple of days, pull another brown bag over the top and store the plants in a cold cellar (with temperatures in the 40s). In early spring, remove them from the bags, clean off the dead leaves, pot them in soil and water well. Prune to desired height. Some of my geraniums have overwintered this way for more than 20 years.

–MRS. HAROLD BEISEL, *Moorefield, Ontario*

I couldn't throw away the poinsettia that my son gave me in 1991, so I came up with a way to keep it thriving and blooming.

It's easy to do, so if you have a leftover poinsettia, consider giving this a try. It's a great challenge.

After the holidays, I keep my poinsettia in a corner of the house near a sunny window. In spring, I plant it in my rock garden when the temperature remains around 50°. I place the plant, pot and all, in a semi-shaded area. Then I bring it back in the house on the first day of autumn.

Once it's back inside, I use a procedure I call "long night, short day" to get it to bloom again. I keep the poinsettia in complete darkness for 14 continuous hours each night. (Either move it to a dark room or closet, or put a box over it.) Continue this treatment until the bracts are fully colored. With these tips, your plant will be beautiful next year for Christmas!

–LORETTA COVERDELL, *Amanda, Ohio*

Every time I water my houseplants, including my prized bonsai, I rotate the pot a quarter turn.

This way new growth comes up evenly, and the plants do not lean in search of light.

–JUDY LARSON, *Greendale, Wisconsin*

Try watering hanging plants with ice cubes.

As the ice melts, the soil absorbs the water, and it doesn't drip out of the bottom of the pot.

–ROSLYN FRANCIS, *Lodi, California*

Tulips are easy to force indoors during winter.

Here's how I keep small houseplants moist while on vacation.

For each plant, I punch a few small holes in a plastic bag. I enclose each plant in a bag and fasten with a twist-tie after watering. The plants stay moist for up to a few weeks.

–LUCILLE RUTH, *Port Charlotte, Florida*

In fall, pot up leftover spring-flowering bulbs, water and store them in a picnic cooler in an unheated garage.

Then, after 12 weeks of cold treatment, bring them indoors and place in a sunny location. They'll start growing and flower in about four weeks.

–HOWARD BASZYNSKI, *Wauwatosa, Wisconsin*

The refrigerator is an easy spot to store seeds over winter. Simply place thoroughly dried seeds collected from your flower and vegetable gardens in envelopes in plastic bags. Label, seal and into the refrigerator they go! Come spring, you'll be all set for planting.

–ELSIE KOLBERG, *St. Joseph, Michigan*

Hang your herbs for drying in winter. Then blend to make your own herb and spice mixes.

year-
rou

Black-capped chickadee

solutions

photo tips

If you have multiple hummingbird feeders in your backyard, you might want to try taking some of them down—except the one you're trying to photograph. This way, you can concentrate hummingbird activity at one particular feeder.

–MIKE MATTHEWS, *Louisville, Kentucky*

Ruby-throated at cardinal flower

Take great hummingbird photos with these tips.

Know your camera. There are a variety of cameras on the market today that will allow you to get great images of hummingbirds. But what's most important is that you take the time to understand your equipment's capabilities, as well as its limitations.

Find support. Tripods are great, but the fast and elusive nature of a hummingbird's flight makes it hard to use one. Instead, I always carry a small towel or beanbag and use it to support my camera. The crook of a tree, windowsill or deck railing can do the job, too. Find a solid surface that works you.

Create the right environment. First of all, you want to make sure you have enough perches for hummingbirds to land, preen and rest. If you don't have many natural perches, make more with dead branches. Next, try to establish your hummingbird area so that the sun is to your back when you observe them. This will allow you to capture greater detail in the feathers.

–**BUD HENSLEY**, *Middleton, Ohio*

Broad-tailed at penstemon

Simple tips to take better **photos**

In the desert when I photograph birds or wildlife, I go back to basics. In other words, I sit in one spot and practice patience. My goal is to become part of the environment. Once you do that, the birds and other wildlife soon go about their normal routines. And this is when you get the best pictures.

–DALE DOMBROWSKI, *Las Vegas, Nevada*

In creating a garden, we provide a wonderful space for all kinds of enchanting creatures. These backyard visitors make great photo subjects!

Photograph butterflies and insects at their eye-level, attempting to get their eyes in sharp focus.

Early morning is the best time for creature photography because cool temperatures usually promote more cooperative subjects.

–NANCY ROTENBERG, *Aliquippa, Pennsylvania*

When you get up close to the flowers you admire from a distance, you start to see details that you might have otherwise missed. For instance, you might see a cool-looking spider or a hidden bird nest with babies in it.

You never know what you might find. There are scenes I most love to capture with my camera. Sometimes this requires a certain amount of stealth, but it's a fun challenge for me. When I'm able to get a shot of something that most people don't take the time to see, or even think to look for, I get to share that special moment in time with everyone else.

–LORI DUNN, *Mount Pleasant Mills, Pennsylvania*

I think the most important part of taking great photos is to learn, practice and never give up. It's critical to have patience.

–JUDY KENNAMER, *Guntersville, Alabama*

Lantana

Buckeye

Hummingbird moth

Early morning is my favorite time to shoot. The light is at its best, and most animals are starting to feed and become active after a night's rest.

–DIANA LE VASSEUR, *Evanston, Wyoming*

Six tips for better flower photos

1. Take pictures early in the morning while the light is soft and before the sun can damage the petals. Don't hesitate to shoot on cloudy days.
2. Use varying angles to get the best point of view. Don't be afraid to shoot the flower from below, beside or behind.
3. Look for the best color combinations. Colors at opposite sides of the color wheel always make great combinations.
4. Use a wide aperture to put the focus on the flower and blur the background.
5. Move in close and use the macro setting on your point-and-shoot camera or a macro lens on your SLR. You'll be amazed at what you see when you get close.
6. Consider buying a polarizing filter to decrease glare in water gardens or a lens hood to prevent lens flare.

–DIANA AUBUCHON, *Overland Park, Kansas*

To give the illusion that birds are in a forest and not your backyard, adorn a feeding tray with various sizes of tree branches.

–JAY FULKERSON, *Woodville, New York*

For fabulous close-up bird photos, use a garage, barn or shed as a photo blind.
I set up several bird feeders and birdbaths near my outbuilding and cut several holes in the wall facing the feeding area.

Make sure the holes are large enough for your camera's lens, and cut each one at a different height. Then place a stool inside near the holes so you can be comfortable while waiting for your feathered friends to take their positions.

–KATHY LOCKWOOD, *St. Johns, Michigan*

The best way to get clear and close bird photos is to use a photo blind.
They can be as simple as a family tent or a covered wooden frame that fits two chairs and a tripod.

–JAY FULKERSON, *Woodville, New York*

If a wild bird flies away when it sees you approach with a camera, don't give up.
Stand still and wait—it'll probably return and accept you in its territory when it feels safe.

–BELINDA NORRIS, *Slater, Missouri*

I set my feeders near brush piles and trees.
This gives me an opportunity to photograph birds in their natural settings as they rest among the branches.

–STANLEY BUMAN, *Carroll, Iowa*

The secret to taking amazing bird photos is to get close.
I found the best way to do this is to use a "bag blind" that drapes over your body. You can buy them or make them out of camouflage fabric. Be sure to cut a hole at the top for your camera lens to fit through. It's the most economical and portable blind I've found.

–PAUL MCAFEE, *Fort Wayne, Indiana*

Birds will stay in your yard longer if you provide a couple of sources of water.
This will give you more chances to take award-winning photographs.

–MARY FARLOW, *Milton, Wisconsin*

Sit near your feeder for a while each time you refill it.
Soon the birds will accept you as part of the landscape. You'll find photographing them will be much easier.

–STEFAN DELLOFF, *Pequannock, New Jersey*

When photographing birds, position yourself and your camera at the level of the subject.
If you see an American robin pulling up a plump worm, lie on your stomach and take the picture from ground level.

–BRANDY LAFOUNTAIN, *Marion, Michigan*

Take several shots of each bird you photograph.
They may unexpectedly turn their head, ruffle their feathers or open their bill mid-shot. Odds are, you'll get a good picture.

–HUBERT BRANDENBURG, *Hagerstown, Maryland*

Pay careful attention to the background of your photograph.
Keep it uncluttered—you may only need to move the camera a few inches to get rid of the distraction. But the extra effort is worth it.

–MARY WELTY, *Denver, North Carolina*

For great hummingbird photos, always cover all but one feeding port at your sugar-water feeder.
I'll use clear marbles or tape to cover the ports. That way, I know exactly where they'll feed and where to focus.

–LEN EISENZIMMER, *Portland, Oregon*

Birds don't pose, so keep shooting.
You'll end up trashing a lot of extra pictures, but it's worth it for a few excellent ones!

–MARY WELTRY, *Denver, North Carolina*

Use a tripod when taking bird photos.

Any camera movement will alter the clarity of your photographs. Zoom and telephoto lenses increase the chances of camera movement.

–TONY SOWERS, *Milo, Iowa*

Indigo bunting

Adding color to a densely shaded area of my garden was easy and inexpensive. I planted three bleeding hearts, three elephant's ear bulbs, two rhododendrons, six lily-of-the-valley plants, three hostas, three ferns, a dozen violets and a flat of impatiens and caladium.

I spent $10 for the flat plus $6 for mulch. The remaining plants—all perennials—came from my yard or from neighbors who traded for other plants.

–JOANNE CRAFT-LANE, *Sumter, South Carolina*

Rhododendron

We surrounded a shady pond on our lot with plenty of hostas. They grow beautifully in the shade.

–**LINDA KOVALCHICK,** *Spokane, Washington*

Here are some of my favorite shade plants: begonias, daylilies, Dutchman's breeches, hydrangeas and bleeding hearts.

–**ANNE THOMPSON,** *Staten Island, New York*

Ferns and hostas are wonderful shade plants. However, we've added impatiens for a splash of color to complement these lush green perennials.

–**KRISTIE STATZ,** *Cross Plains, Wisconsin*

Use wax begonias in shade gardens. They provide nice leaf contrast and pretty flowers.

–**JACKIE EGERTON,** *Reisterstown, Maryland*

Want a better garden?

Try these reader-tested tips.

Working soil that is too wet can actually cause long-term damage.

Squeeze a handful of soil—if it crumbles through your fingers, you're ready to garden. Otherwise, give it a few days to dry.

–B. ROSIE LERNER, *Purdue University*

I hate to weed my garden.

Several years ago, I read a book that suggested using wheat straw around plants to contain weeds. Now I'm a big fan of wheat straw, and I use it all around my plants. It keeps away unwanted foliage, enriches the soil and helps my plants retain water. Plus, its golden color looks beautiful in the garden. It's the best mulch I've ever used, so I love to share this tip with other gardeners.

–MELANIE DEAN, *Assumption, Minnesota*

Don't cover a tree's roots with dirt to add flowers because it can damage the tree.

We encircled a silver maple with cinder blocks. Each block was filled with potting soil and four impatiens plants. Before we knew it, the shady spot was full of color, and it wasn't really expensive. Best of all, our tree is still healthy, too.

–RON AND JULIE KULA, *Central City, Nebraska*

My yard was plagued with dandelions.

I spent a fortune on weed killer until I found something in my kitchen that worked—salt and vinegar. Mix 1 part salt to 3 parts vinegar, heat until it's warm, and then cool and pour into a spray bottle. This also kills other plants, so use sparingly and with caution.

–DEBBIE HEATON, *Toccoa, Georgia*

I had a real garden challenge—finding something to add color

under the shady canopy of five large maple trees.

So I finally tried impatiens. They were the perfect solution and bloomed like crazy.

–MONICA MEULEMANS, *Wrightstown, Wisconsin*

Got a favorite flower patch with poor soil?

Know a place where fishermen buy worms? Bring home that rich black dirt and a bunch of worms and sprinkle them into the problem patch. After one season, this will enrich and aerate even the most problematic soil and produce healthy flowers.

–GERALD MCLAUGHLIN, *New Castle, Pennsylvania*

My garden used to be filled with weeds.

Then, a couple of years ago, when I had boxes left over from moving, I got the idea to bury cardboard around my garden plants. I covered it with wood chips from a local tree company. Now my garden is a lot easier to weed and it doesn't require as much water. Cardboard is easy to obtain—try an appliance dealer. Just watch out for staples, and don't use any waxed cardboard.

–ALEX THURLOW, *Brooklyn, Connecticut*

To kill dandelions in my strawberry patch,

I cut both ends from a 2-liter bottle, place it over the weed and spray with Roundup (or other total vegetation killers that do not stay in the soil). This keeps the herbicide off the strawberries and kills the weeds.

–RALPH SUMMERS, *Mountain Grove, Missouri*

I am a firm believer in mulching with hay.

I've found it makes weeding easier—which is kinder to my knees and back. We use it on our garden pathways, in the vegetable garden and around border plants.

I like to put down a layer 4 to 5 inches thick. It will settle down with the first rain and after a little foot traffic. The next spring, I put a fresh layer right over the top of the old hay, and then once more if we have a really wet summer.

I've found that hay readily decomposes, unlike bark mulch. And I haven't encountered any problems with stray seeds from the hay growing in the garden. All I see is a healthy garden that I can easily walk around and view up close.

–PEGGY MOEN, *Foxboro, Wisconsin*

Glory-of-the-snow

I plant forget-me-nots, violets and myrtle in a shady corner of our lot. The plants are surrounded by a lovely backdrop of scotch pines.

–ROSE WHIPPLE
Oneida, New York

Plant white impatiens in a shady garden to make it bright and noticeable. The white flowers look nice at night, too.

–PATRICIA ERNST
Cincinnati, Ohio

Lazy gardening is my specialty! I've always had trouble with our clay soil, so I found an easy remedy. I buy as much good compost as I can afford, and then I spread it out over areas in my yard where I want to plant. Then I water the area regularly, as if plants were already there.

Within a few months, the organic matter has trickled down to the soil. And as I dig in to plant my new garden, I have a good mix of compost. If you do this a few months before you want to start your garden, the area will be ready just in time.

–JENNIFER IFVERSEN
Albuquerque, New Mexico

American painted lady
on coneflower

Consider making a winding path through shady areas. A path alone will create interest, giving a woodsy feel. I added shade-loving perennials along my path and a bench for enjoying its solitude.

–**JUDY HOOLSEMA**, *Portage, Michigan*

I mix a small amount of leftover "juice" from our pickle jars with water and pour it on my flowering shrubs. It gives my soil some acidity and makes my flowering shrubs bloom more profusely.

–**SANDRA PARKER**, *Glen Burnie, Maryland*

I bring color to my shady yard by hanging baskets of impatiens. There are other advantages to these baskets, too. Hummingbirds enjoy impatiens, and the hungry critters that eat the flowers planted in my yard can't reach them.

–**RICHARD WALTERS**, *North Myrtle Beach, South Carolina*

hat could be more inviting than artfully landscaped garden?

critter control

Gray squirrel

To make a squirrel-proof bird feeder for me, my cousin drilled holes in the bottom of plastic water bottles, threaded them onto a small cable and added a pulley in the middle. Then he attached the cable between two trees and ran another small cable through the middle pulley, attached to the bird feeder. This allows me to lower the feeder for easy filling.

When squirrels try to get to the feeder, they spin off the water bottles, leaving the birdseed for birds to enjoy.

–LARRY DECET, *Trimble, Missouri*

To keep the raccoons off our feeders, we attached stovepipe around the base. Then we painted flowers all over the new pipes. Now we have a great feeding area that is pretty to look at and keeps the critters away. I haven't seen a single raccoon on my feeder since!

–MADGE MARTINSON, *Durand, Michigan*

The squirrels used to empty my mesh bird feeder within hours until I discovered this simple deterrent. One day, I hooked a shepherd's hook over a tree branch instead of placing it in the ground, then hung the feeder on it as I normally would. When a squirrel hops on, it throws off the balance of the hook, and the squirrel falls off.

–JEAN LEITNER, *Turin, New York*

Red squirrel

To combat squirrels, we put a chimney pipe around the pole that held the bird feeder, which kept most of them off. But there was still a small squirrel that was able to jump to the frame, so we screwed 9-by-12-inch pieces of Plexiglas around the sides. It was kind of funny to watch the squirrel struggle before finally giving up.

–BETSY ERNST, *Nunica, Michigan*

Bunnies are cute, but not when they're in my vegetable garden. After trying numerous methods to lure them away from my veggies, I found one that worked best: I planted marigolds around the perimeter of the vegetable garden.

To my surprise, the rabbits don't go near my garden anymore. I don't know if this will work for everyone, but it sure does the trick for me.

–DEBORAH PETERSEN, *Willmar, Minnesota*

Place thorny clippings at the base of bird feeders. Squirrels will try to cross once, but only once. They'll quickly learn to leave your feeder alone and try someplace else.

–CHARLOTTE HUTCHESON, *Gainesville, Georgia*

I have tried all types of baffles and guards in the past to keep squirrels off the bird feeders, but to no avail. Until now, that is. Simply drill a hole in the bottom of a plastic planter and slip it on the pole top down below the feeder, fastening it with a clamp. Then sit back and watch as the squirrels try to climb the pole. They'll wonder what's going on as their paws slide off the planter, and down they go!

–DOROTHY ODETTE, *Longville, Minnesota*

To prevent squirrels from pigging out at my bird feeders, I make little treats to keep them occupied. I call them Fur 'n' Feather Peanut Butter Cups. All you need are several individual applesauce cups, one 40-ounce jar of chunky peanut butter and some wild birdseed. After you enjoy the applesauce yourself, put the birdseed and peanut butter into the empty cups and put them in the freezer. When the squirrels need a distraction, pop one out and set it well away from your bird feeders. The squirrels will love their frozen treat.

–HELEN GOODWIN, *Winter Park, Florida*

To keep deer, rabbits and raccoons out of our garden and sweet corn, we bought a bottle of liquid coyote scent at our local hunting and fishing store.

We tied cotton balls with thread and hung them from stakes around the garden, then put a few drops of the scent on each one. The animals think there are coyotes near and will not come close to the garden.

–CAROL POTTER, *Salem, Indiana*

Do you have problems keeping the house sparrows out of your bluebird boxes? Our bird expert has a solution. George Harrison first recommends placing the birdhouse at the edge of an open field where the habitat is better for bluebirds. Also, make sure the entrance holes aren't too big. If that doesn't work, you can legally remove the nests because they're not native.

if you spend hours battling squirrels in your backyard it's time to **try these reader tricks!**

I have built many birdhouses over the years, and I've learned how to keep squirrels from destroying the entrances. I attach a flat steel washer around the entrance hole, either 1 ¼ inches of 1 ½ inches, depending on what type of bird will inhabit the house.

–**ROY M. SEPPALA,** *Pembroke, Massachusetts*

Squirrels don't eat our birdseed anymore, and all it took was a little height. My husband simply hung our tray feeder 12 feet off the ground. Now it's just above eye level when we sit on our deck. We live in the mountains, where there's plenty of wildlife all around us. Our birds can eat in peace now, and we're delighted that we have the perfect view to enjoy all our feathered friends.

–**MARIAN BACKENSTOES,** *Manheim, Pennsylvania*

Squirrels used to empty and ruin my bird feeders until I started putting a couple of scoops of sunflower seeds under the pine tree for them. Now the squirrels eat their seeds and leave my feeders alone.

–**DELORIS BOWEN,** *Columbia, Connecticut*

I have a very simple solution to the problem of squirrels raiding bird feeders. I fill three old containers with sunflower seeds and place them around my yard, near my feeders. The squirrels love the sunflower seeds, and they would rather take an easy meal on the ground than climb up on the feeders.

–**JENNIE GRAVATT,** *Salina, Kansas*

You don't need commercial products to keep deer away. Just sprinkle your garden with a mixture of crushed garlic, garlic powder and dill pickle juice. Your neighbors might think you're cooking spaghetti, but the deer don't care for the scent.

–**JEN WOOD,** *Newfane, Vermont*

A hanging birdbath makes a great feeder. Instead of water, I fill it with birdseed. To keep squirrels away, cut a piece of hardware cloth slightly larger than the feeder. Bend the wire mesh over the sides of the dish so it's secure.

–**JILL MCKEE-KELSO,** *Chula Vista, California*

I enjoy watching the mourning doves on my patio, but I don't like seeing sparrows or squirrels stealing all the seed. To keep pests out, I made a simple feeder. I started with a wooden frame and then attached ¼-inch galvanized hardware cloth to the top. The doves can easily reach in, but the squirrels and sparrows stay out. It's the perfect ground feeder, and now I don't have to worry about my birdseed disappearing so fast.

–**DAVID HUNTER,** *Champaign, Illinois*

To keep squirrels from climbing feeder poles, we've used motor grease. It's messy but effective.

–**GORDON PRICE,** *Dayton, Ohio*

After years of feeding birds, this is the only squirrel-proof solution we've found. We cut the neck off a 2-liter soda bottle and slipped it on the pole below the feeder. It really works for us!

–**LENORE MATHER,** *Waverly, New York*

I have a feeder system that works wonders. A squirrel has yet to conquer it. Here's my secret.

I hang all of my feeders from trolling wire, the kind typically used for fishing. I use 50-pound test wire because of its strength and durability. Plus, the squirrels can't bite through it.

My system works best for the lightweight feeders. The squirrels can't get the food, so they eat the seeds that fall to the ground.

–**DOREEN PUGH,** *Manhasset, New York*

A single corncob can go a long way. To keep squirrels fed and away from my bird feeders, I set out whole ears of corn. When the squirrels are finished eating the corn, I spread the cob with peanut butter and roll it in birdseed. Then I twist wire around the end and hang it from a nail on my deck. The birds love it.

–**LORRENE PIERSON,** *Marionville, Missouri*

We were having trouble with the squirrels and raccoons at our bird feeder, so we designed a circular tier to keep them away. We are now raccoon- and squirrel-free, and the tier keeps the area under our feeder clean. We use the fallen seed to feed the deer in our yard.

–**KEN AND MARIEROSE RONYCK,** *Winnipeg, Manitoba*

Gray squirrel

Even more tips to **combat squirrels**

After 15 years of fighting pesky critters, I finally found a way to squirrel-proof a bird feeder. I loosely attached a wok facedown above the feeder so that it hung over like a roof. It sways easily side to side, so when squirrels jump on it to try and get to the feeder, the roof swings away and the squirrel falls to the ground.

–**LEE HODGES**, *Grants Pass, Oregon*

If raccoons and skunks get into your sweet corn, surround the patch with winter squash or pumpkins. As the vines grow, train them around the outside of the patch so they overlap. This trick has worked for me for years. It's also a convenient way to grow space-consuming vine crops.

–**PAT NELSON**, *Cody, Wyoming*

We have lots of oak trees in our area, and unfortunately that means a lot of squirrels, too. Our bird feeders are prime targets for these critters, so I wanted to stop them from stealing all of our birdseed. I took five plastic bottles and drilled 1-inch holes in the caps and bottoms. Then I slipped them onto the pipe that holds our feeder. The squirrels no longer steal my birdseed!

–**LA MOTTE BRINDLEY**, *Lorain, Ohio*

I hang my bird feeders directly below our patio roof. The squirrels can't jump or climb to them, and it brings the birds in really close.

–**MARY EM MCGLONE**

Philadelphia, Pennsylvania

Hang small wind chimes from the bottom of your bird feeders. The sound of the chimes frightens squirrels but doesn't bother the birds.

–**CAROL DRAPER**, *Little Rock, Arkansas*

Red squirrel

Opossum

One year the critters in my backyard really challenged me. The chipmunks and deer wouldn't leave my plants alone. Then I discovered peppermint oil. Not only did putting it on my plants work, but my entire yard smelled great.

The only problem, as I discovered, is that you have to reapply the peppermint oil after each rain. It's still my favorite thing to keep critters out, though.

–DORIS MILLER, *Libertyville, Illinois*

I have a quick solution to keep squirrels away from my bird feeders. I use 6-inch furnace pipes, snapped together around the regular feeder pole.

When I first tried this out, the squirrels climbed and climbed but couldn't make any progress up the slick metal. Since it worked so well, I added two more pipes to my other feeders. This is an easy and inexpensive solution that you can get from any home improvement store. It keeps the squirrels at bay and leaves birdseed for the birds.

–JIM SOLAZZO, *Mt. Prospect, Illinois*

For many years, I had a problem with raccoons eating my birdseed. I tried putting the feeder on a pole, in a tree and several other places, but nothing worked. Then, last year, I finally found the answer to this dilemma.

I used a plastic gallon milk jug, cut holes in two sides, ran a wire through the lid and hung it from the porch ceiling. It took a few days for the birds to find it, but they did. Once I discovered that the birds loved it, I made more. There's no way the raccoons could climb up the wall and across the ceiling.

–SUSAN REYNOLDS, *Ferdinand, Indiana*

Potato beetle larva

Crop rotation is one of the best weapons against garden pests.

–MARJORIE CAREY, *Freeport, Florida*

Cover cabbage heads with nylons to keep out the white moth or butterfly that produces green worms.

–**ELLEN GAUGLER**, *Hoselaw, Alberta*

White-crowned sparrow

I keep destructive insects out of my garden by relying on backyard birds. In spring, I turn in all my leaves with a spade and wait for the robins, sparrows, blackbirds and wrens to arrive to feast on the insects.

–MAE WARRICK, *Jennings, Kansas*

Cicada

To get rid of pests, keep a bottle of rubbing alcohol on hand in your garden shed. It's a cheap and easy way to reduce aphids, leafhoppers, mealybugs, spider mites and whiteflies.

Mix ½ cup of rubbing alcohol with a quart of water and lightly mist infected plants. Test first on a leaf to make sure there is no damage.

–MARY MILLER, *Clayton, Illinois*

I like to keep a bar of soap in my watering can. When I water my plants, they get a dose of anti-bug soap in the process.

–SUSIE FISHER, *Lewistown, Pennsylvania*

I've achieved good insect control by planting garlic and marigolds in every garden row. I alternate the two, planting one or the other every 3 feet or so.

–YOLI QUEVEDO, *Anacortes, Washington*

Grasshopper

Instead of spraying for whiteflies, we paint sticks of wood yellow, then smear them with petroleum jelly. The flies are attracted to the color and get stuck in the jelly.

–ELIZABETH SRUTOWSKI
Mesa, Arizona

Plant dill with all your vine crops. This versatile herb does extra duty in repelling squash bugs and cucumber beetles.

–KAREN ANN BLAND
Gove, Kansas

Potato beetle

To reduce the bug population, we make our yard inviting to the birds that eat lots of insects. We planted mountain ash, honeysuckle, crabapples and a Juneberry tree. We also have a bird feeder and two birdbaths next to the garden.

–AZALEA WRIGHT
Forest Lake, Minnesota

Cutworms have been nuisances in my garden for years. My family has passed on this classic tip to keep them away: Simply put two nails at the base of your tomatoes or other young plants. This simple trick helps keep cutworms from destroying your crop.

–JOE LAMOREX
Leeburg, Georgia

To protect plants from cutworms, sprinkle a ring of cornmeal around each plant.

–WANDA BURRER
Wing, North Dakota

To protect fruit from insects, hang small cans of sugar-water from the branches. The bugs and insects will be drawn to the cans instead of the fruit.

–JANET WATSON
De Motte, Indiana

Summer tanager

Nothing stops cutworms better than this simple collar. Remove the bottom from a foam cup, slit one side and place around the plant, with cut sides overlapping. Push the cup into the soil to keep it from blowing over.

–WELDON BURGE, *Newark, Delaware*

Plant two or three dill seeds in each squash hill, and you won't have any squash bugs.

–DEE HANCOCK, *Fremont, Nebraska*

To keep box elder bugs away from the warm side of your house in spring and fall, mix liquid dishwashing soap and water in a spray bottle. Spray the side and base of the house, repeating if necessary.

–MONICA BENGSTON, *Independence, Iowa*

Put a short length of hose in your garden to control earwigs. They will crawl inside, and you can drop the hose into a shallow bucket of water to rinse them out and then destroy them.

–JUDIE WILKINSON, *Escondido, California*

Place 1 teaspoon of sugar and 1 teaspoon of powdered boric acid in a covered jar. Make holes in the top large enough for ants to enter. They take the mixture back to their nest. Soon you won't have an ant problem.

–HELEN COSTELLO, *Chicopee, Massachusetts*

To protect garden plants from slugs, spread a layer of crushed eggshells around them.

–MARIE BLAHUT, *Yorkton, Saskatchewan*

To keep flies away, plant savory in pots next to your house. Flies don't like the smell. Living on a farm with livestock close by, we've tried this many times, and it works.

–ROXANN BISTLINE, *Brandon, Iowa*

Bothered by hornets, wasps and bees? I'm allergic to their stings, so hanging moth cakes on our deck has been a lifesaver. We also put them under the eaves—anywhere there might be nests. They don't like the smell and fly far away to build their nests.

–MARGARET LINDOW, *Suamico, Wisconsin*

To keep ants out of the house, sprinkle a solid line of kitchen cleanser along the door sill. One application at our patio entrance and front door lasted at least three years. Low-cost generic products are the best, because they are more grainy than name brands.

–ALICE GOSLOW, *Clinton Township, Michigan*

For slugs, fill shallow plates or small cans with honey or yeast and place in the soil, with the opening at ground level. The slugs will crawl in and die.

–MARY STAGER, *Silver Bay, Minnesota*

Here's a cheap, natural way to repel aphids and spider mites. Mix 1/3 cup cooking oil and 1 teaspoon baking soda in a jar; keep covered until needed. Combine 2 teaspoons of mixture with 1 cup water in a sprayer.

–HENRYETTE MARSHALL, *Jensen Beach, Florida*

For the past two years, I've planted garlic cloves 2 to 3 feet apart in each row of potatoes, and I haven't had any potato bugs.

–RUBY SACCONE, *Clarksburg, West Virginia*

I mix equal amounts of vinegar and water and spray it on slugs. They dissolve instantly.

–MILDRED BRITTON, *Glendale, California*

To prevent slug damage to tomatoes, circle plants with a layer of cornmeal about 1/8 inch thick and about 3 inches away from the plant's stem.

–GLORIA TJERNLUND, *Ironwood, Michigan*

Lemons will discourage ants from entering your home. Just put lemon slices around your doorway or wherever ants are getting in. Within two hours, they should be gone.

–KATHRYN GEMMILL, *York Springs, Pennsylvania*

Mosquitoes chew me up whenever I work in the garden. So I mix 1 tablespoon of Murphy's Oil Soap with a gallon of water. Then I put it in a spray bottle and spritz between the rows where I want to work. This mixture can also be sprayed around bushes, picnic tables, swings and seating areas. It really drives the mosquitoes away.

–MARIE BAKER, *Decatur, Indiana*

make it for less

I love to use recycled items to build things for my backyard. For example, I made a sunflower decoration from rotary hoe pickers, steel fence posts and an old plow disk for the base. It's a fun accent for my yard, and it always sparks a conversation when people visit.

–EDWARD DURLER, *Dodge City, Kansas*

Why buy a gardening kneeling pad when a piece of old carpet padding will suffice? Just cut a "handle"—an oval-shaped hole at one end—to carry it around.

–POLLY KELLY, *Birmingham, Alabama*

Instead of buying a garden tool wagon or bag, I purchased an old golf bag for $5 at a flea market. I use it to haul my garden tools around the yard, which eliminates wasted trips back and forth to my garage. The bag is just tall enough to accommodate my long-handled tools and keep them organized and easy to reach. The pockets are perfect for twine, clippers, seed packets and pruning shears.

–LINDA VIZZA, *Peterborough, Ontario*

I love the beautiful metal hose guards that I see in stores, but they're very expensive. So I started picking up old fireplace tool sets from thrift stores for an average of $3 each. Then I cut off the shovel, brush and poker with a hacksaw, which leaves me with a set of three guards to use wherever I need to protect my flower beds from a hose. I've found some with very interesting handles that are just as attractive as those I see in the catalogs.

–INEZ RABIDEAU, *Appleton, Wisconsin*

Instead of buying plant stakes, I use small straight limbs that fall from trees. They blend into my garden and are a lot cheaper.

–LINDY RICHEE, *Burbank, Illinois*

Used golf club shafts (without club heads) are very handy in the garden. I get mine from golf pro shops and repair shops. I use them to stake pepper plants, mark my rows and even support young trees.

–LARRY DEROCHE, *Dunstable, Massachusetts*

I save all my old shoestrings and soft fabric belts. That way, I always have something on hand whenever I need to tie up flowers and tomato plants that need some support.

–JANET LUSCH, *Vandalia, Illinois*

I found a practical use for my old satellite dish: I transformed it into a birdbath by attaching it to the top of my chain-link fence with a hose clamp.

–REBECCA LEE, *High Rolls, New Mexico*

Make finch feeders from plastic poster tubes. I cut them to 14 inches long, poke a tiny feeding hole about 4 inches from the bottom, and drill a larger hole through the entire tube a couple of inches below it.

Insert a wooden dowel into the large hole as a perch and cap both ends of the tube. Your feeder is complete. I attract lots of finches with these homemade feeders.

–VANESSA MOW, *Farmington, Pennsylvania*

We've had a lot of trees fall down because of storms. So we make use of them by cutting the trunks into slices. They make pretty steppingstones.

–DEANE TAYLOR, *Summerfield, North Carolina*

The finches love the feeder I designed. I made it using materials I had around the house.

With a 1/16-inch drill bit, I made a hole in the bottom of a 20-ounce plastic bottle so my feathered friends could feed. Then I screwed the bottle onto scrap wood and attached dowel pieces for perches. I put a screw eye through the cap for easy hanging. It was a cinch to make, and best of all, it's easy to clean.

–ROY HIXSON, *New Carlisle, Ohio*

I love watching the American goldfinches at my feeder, but I thought there had to be a way to stop wasting all the seed that was falling under my deck and through the floor cracks.

In my basement, I found an unused paint tray that fit perfectly over my deck railing just below the feeder. Now the finches have an extra feeding place inside the tray, and no seed is wasted.

–VIOLET COUNTRYMAN, *Tillsonburg, Ontario*

I stumbled upon an old unwanted satellite dish, so I came up with an idea to recycle it. I made it into a pond. It cost a total of $50 for the water pump and took a little bit of work, but it's the best use I've seen for one of those old things.

–PAT RICE, *Mukwonago, Wisconsin*

The weather in northeastern Colorado can make nurturing young plants and seedlings a challenge in the spring. But one day while walking around my yard, it occurred to me that my two large south-facing window wells would make perfect mini greenhouses for my young plants.

To protect them, I placed a vinyl shower curtain over the top and secured it with large rocks. Now I just have to keep an eye on them when it's cold, but the hardening-off process is much easier on my plants— and simpler for me.

–LAURA SCHUCK, *Loveland, Colorado*

Our new home needed a window bird feeder, so I set out to make one. I found an empty CD case, the kind that holds 10 disks, in my desk drawer. I took a woodburning pen and melted holes in the plastic for suction cups.

I opened the case and taped the corners so the sides would be at a 90-degree angle, leaving the CD pocket upright to hold the seed. Finally, I added drainage holes. With a few simple tools, you can make a window feeder, too!

–LORETTA GRUNEWALD, *Elkton, Virginia*

My husband builds birdhouses and feeders for friends and relatives. He buys old shovels and pitchforks at garage sales, then attaches small houses and feeders to the handles. He leaves his creations unpainted for folks to decorate themselves, if they desire. Best of all, they can be easily moved around the yard.

–KATHY CAPANNA, *Springfield, Oregon*

For an inexpensive suet feeder, put a block of suet inside a nylon hairnet. Once you tie the top and hang it, you have an instant feeder. The birds love it, and it's very "cheep"!
—SARA SUNDBY, *Thief River Falls, Minnesota*

Common redpolls

This old shovel gets a new life, thanks to a little bit of paint. Opposite page, innovative containers also use recycled objects.

WELCOME

When our granddaughters visited us one summer, we made a rocking chair garden together. My husband dug an old chair out of a trash bin, and I painted it and added their names. They picked out the flowers and planted them. It was fun to share gardening with them.

–LINDA BROWN
Germantown, Ohio

I've seen pictures of bottle trees for years and finally decided to make my own. My husband made my vision come to life by welding rebar together. My tree holds a total of 47 bottles and stands 8 feet high.

–LISA ELDRED
Battle Creek, Michigan

You can make an easy and inexpensive bird feeding tower from concrete cinder blocks. Stack the blocks with the holes facing out. Then place different types of birdseed in each compartment. You can create your own design. I added a large pan to the top of my stack that serves as a birdbath.

–SUE SAYRE
Milan, Missouri

I turned an ordinary frying pan into a simple birdbath. I set it in a thick patch of pampas grass to provide protective cover. The birds flock to it.

–LYDIA POST, *Parchment, Michigan*

I couldn't find any hose hideaways that I liked, so I made my own from a discarded tire.

With a sharp utility knife, I cut about 3 inches off at the rim bead on one side. Then I applied two coats of good latex house paint, decorated it with flowers and drilled four holes in the underside for drainage. This bowl stores about 200 feet of 5/8-inch hose.

–OREON WESCHE, *Overland, Missouri*

I buy old bowling balls for my garden at yard sales and thrift shops. I put them hole side down, sometimes on the base of a birdbath. Pearlized or marbled ones look best. A marbled red, white and blue ball on a cobalt stand is my favorite. I've never spent more than $5 for these lawn ornaments, and they never break, fade—or move!

–CHRISTINE PINNELL, *Stockbridge, Georgia*

I recycled my mother's mailbox by placing it in my garden, where it now serves as a handy little garden shed. Inside it, I keep a trowel, clippers and extra gardening gloves.

–TAMALA BIGGER, *St. Clair, Michigan*

We needed a new grill. But before we threw the old one out, I realized I could make a great potting table by simply removing the hood and doors. Instead of throwing away the doors, I placed them on top of the table to make a flat work surface. It's really handy, and the wheels allow it to move easily around my yard.

–PEGGY BASILE, *Sanford, Maine*

I live in a condo but have the privilege of maintaining a little flower garden. At times, the lawn mower would cross over into my garden, so I placed some pieces of leftover ceramic tile around it to serve as a border. It really helps define the space and keeps the lawn mower from ruining my flowers.

–JOAN WALTON, *Cedar Rapids, Iowa*

I made my own hand-held hummingbird feeder.

I took a plastic drink bottle and cut off the top part, leaving the cap attached. Then I drew a flower petal design around the cap, cutting off the excess plastic.

I cut out another bottle top, gluing one end of a small PVC pipe to the inside of it and the other end to the inside of the other cap. Next, I drilled a hole through the second cap. Then I painted the whole thing red and filled it with nectar. It works like a charm. You just sit still and wait, and the hummingbirds will come!

–RONALD HALL, *Salley, South Carolina*

Old spatulas and spoons make great plant markers.

I find them at rummage sales and discount stores for less than 25 cents each. Use a fine-tip permanent marker to write the plant name on the front of the utensil and the planting date on the back. If you want to reuse them the next season, use a scrubbing pad to remove the writing.

–LINDA RAMSEY, *Chelsea, Oklahoma*

When I replaced the shutters on my house, I put the old ones to good use as frames for a raised bed.

They were the perfect size, 4 feet by 1 foot. I enclosed the ends with scrap lumber. It fit a narrow area in my yard just right and matches the trim on my house.

–DIANE JOHNSON, *Hutchinson, Minnesota*

I found a way to make a handheld hummingbird feeder from household items.

Glue a piece of red fabric or a red plastic flower to the top of a film canister and pierce a hole though both the fabric or flower and lid. Fill the canister with sugar water, cap it up and remove your usual hummingbird feeder. Then stand still and wait for the hummingbirds to discover the treat.

–BETTY PIERCE, *Slaterville Springs, New York*

During the summer, I use rain barrels to collect water for my flowers.

They fill up almost all the way in just a few minutes after a brief shower. To make one, cut your downspout slightly higher than the height of a trash can. Then, using a utility knife, cut an opening into the lid of the can that accommodates the downspout.

–LEE KLINE, *Leesburg, Florida*

I had little money for landscaping when I bought my house in 1990, so I took every opportunity to recycle others' "trash."

When my boss got a new driveway, I asked him for the old concrete. I used a sledgehammer to break up the pieces. Then I dug out a path, placing the concrete pieces in to create a stone walkway.

–CHRIS JOHNSON, *Boise, Idaho*

I often divide my perennials in fall and replant the divisions in my gardens.

But by spring, I've completely forgotten where to expect them and I sometimes disturb the area. Labeling the plants was the obvious solution, but everything I tried faded, disappeared or looked unnatural.

Finally I hit on using rocks. I collect them on walks and bike rides, wash them and keep them in a handy pile. If I'm in a hurry, I simply print the plant's name with black enamel paint and cover with varnish. If I'm feeling artistic, I paint a picture of its blossom, too. It's also a welcome surprise when sharing a plant with a friend to include a labeled rock.

–MARY ELLEN WYNES, *Mount Pleasant, Michigan*

The rain barrels I was shopping for were so expensive I decided to make my own.

The total cost for it was under $70: $50 for the urn and under $17 for the fittings, epoxy, faucet and elbows.

–EVERETT HATTON, *Edgewater, Florida*

I use old tires to make raised flower beds.

Just take a roofing or utility knife and remove one sidewall by cutting it near the tread. Then place the tire upside down wherever you want your new flower bed. The tire will help hold in moisture, so you won't need to water the plants as frequently.

–NAOMI OCHS, *Independence, Missouri*

House sparrow

My friend Harold Lyon and I are retired recyclers who love birds. We use old materials like lanterns, light fixtures and teakettles to make bird feeders. It's a great way to recycle what normally would end up in the trash, and the birds love them!

–DAVE PROUTY, *Wausau, Wisconsin*

meet the photographers

Marie Read is an acclaimed wildlife photographer based near Ithaca, New York, whose photos and articles are featured regularly in magazines, calendars, books and other publications worldwide. She has traveled widely in search of photo subjects, from Florida and California to Australia, Kenya and Panama. But she's found many of her most memorable images in her own backyard or within a couple of miles of her home. She has written two books: *Common Birds and Their Songs* (co-authored with sound recordist Lang Elliott) and *Secret Lives of Common Birds*, both published by Houghton Mifflin.

Terry Wild, from Williamsport, Pennsylvania, has been a photographer for more than 40 years. He established the Terry Wild Studio in 1974 and worked as a commercial photographer from 1974 to 2000, specializing in education, finance and health subjects. In 2000, he established Terry Wild Stock, a searchable online database picture agency that works with regional and national publications. Now his favorite photography subjects are our lands, skies, flora, fauna, structures, and those who work with the planet to help make it greener.

Carol L. Edwards, a freelance nature photographer from Ontario, specializes in images of birds and wildlife. She grew up in Owen Sound, in the beautiful Georgian Bay area, where she now roams the backroads and nature trails with a DSLR camera paired with a powerful telephoto lens. Before becoming a professional photographer recognized for intimate images of birds and butterflies that often tell a story, she was an avid gardener. She is transforming her urban property into a bird and butterfly haven and creating a backyard nature studio.

Steve (pictured) and Dave Maslowski of Cincinnati have a combined seven decades of photography experience. They learned much of their craft from their father, the late Karl Maslowski, who started his wildlife photography enterprise in the 1930s. Since then, technological advancements have radically changed virtually every aspect of animal photography. The one thing that hasn't changed is the brothers' goal of producing interesting pictures that convey aspects of their subjects' behavior and habits. Steve and Dave have English degrees from Brown University and the University of Cincinnati, respectively.

Bill Johnson was born and raised in Excelsior, Minnesota, and now lives in Minneapolis. He's been a stock photographer for the past 18 years, but his interest in taking photos started when he was a young boy. Bill specializes in plant and insect photography but also photographs birds, mammals, reptiles and a number of habitats ranging from deserts to swamps. Bill has contributed to more than 20 national magazines and is a charter member of the North American Nature Photography Association, as well as a member of the Garden Writers Association.

Everything has its beauty,
but not everyone sees it.